Regulation, Compliance and Ethics in Law Firms

Tracey Calvert

SECOND EDITION

Globe Law and Business

Author
Tracey Calvert

Managing director
Sian O'Neill

Regulation, Compliance and Ethics in Law Firms, Second Edition
is published by

Globe Law and Business Ltd
3 Mylor Close
Horsell
Woking
Surrey GU21 4DD
United Kingdom
Tel: +44 20 3745 4770
www.globelawandbusiness.com

Printed and bound by CPI Group (UK) Ltd, Croydon CR0 4YY, United Kingdom

Regulation, Compliance and Ethics in Law Firms

ISBN 9781787423787
EPUB ISBN 9781787423794
Adobe PDF ISBN 9781787423800
Mobi ISBN 9781787423817

© 2020 Globe Law and Business Ltd except where otherwise indicated.

The right of Tracey Calvert to be identified as author of this work has been asserted by her in accordance with sections 77 and 78 of the Copyright, Designs and Patents Act 1988.

Extracts from the Handbook, the Standards and Regulations and the Statement of Solicitor Competence, SRA guidance and other regulatory materials are reproduced with the kind permission of the Law Society.

All rights reserved. No part of this publication may be reproduced in any material form (including photocopying, storing in any medium by electronic means or transmitting) without the written permission of the copyright owner, except in accordance with the provisions of the Copyright, Designs and Patents Act 1988 or under terms of a licence issued by the Copyright Licensing Agency Ltd, 6–10 Kirby Street, London EC1N 8TS, United Kingdom (www.cla.co.uk, email: licence@cla.co.uk). Applications for the copyright owner's written permission to reproduce any part of this publication should be addressed to the publisher.

DISCLAIMER
This publication is intended as a general guide only. The information and opinions which it contains are not intended to be a comprehensive study, or to provide legal advice, and should not be treated as a substitute for legal advice concerning particular situations. Legal advice should always be sought before taking any action based on the information provided. The publishers bear no responsibility for any errors or omissions contained herein.

Table of contents

Preface _____ 5

Section 1: Governance and risk management _____ 9

Introduction _____ 9
   Chapter 1: Effective law firm management _____ 11

Section 2: Demonstrating regulatory compliance in practice ___ 73

Introduction _____ 73
   Chapter 2: What is ethics? _____ 81
   Chapter 3: Essential behaviour _____ 85
   Chapter 4: Evidence of compliance _____ 115
   Chapter 5: Safe client inception processes _____ 121
   Chapter 6: Compliance in the litigation arena _____ 131
   Chapter 7: Adding the people and commercial _____ 147
   perspective to regulatory standards
   Chapter 8: The Legal Ombudsman – why are we bothered? ___ 153

Section 3: Compliance with legal obligations _____ 165

Introduction _____ 165
   Chapter 9: An overview of legal compliance _____ 169

Chapter 10: Managing the money laundering risk	177
Chapter 11: Managing the risks of handling data	197

Section 4: Compliance tools and resources _____ 205

Introduction _____ 205

Chapter 12: Be aware of recent changes	209
Chapter 13: Remote working – compliance considerations	215
Chapter 14: Conclusion	227
Chapter 15: Resources	235

Notes _____ 237

About the author _____ 241

Index _____ 243

About Globe Law and Business _____ 249

Preface

Why regulation, compliance and ethics matter
Why has the legal profession thrived despite all the pressures of twenty-first century business? With the competition from other legal services providers, the ability of users to access information on the internet, and the do-it-yourself lawyering that is possible, why is the solicitor's profession still in existence?

The quick answer comes with an easy to understand concept: the majority of consumers have confidence in us and our profession. The more detailed answer includes an explanation as to why this is so, and with this it is necessary to consider the constraints within which we must operate when we provide services to consumers.

The constraints are imposed on us through the regulatory and legal standards we must meet and the professional ethics we must display. Both are achieved through compliance.

Some critics of this trio of requirements – regulation, compliance and ethics – including some lawyers with whom you may share office space, will suggest that they are unnecessary and expensive additional burdens. However, it is the view of the author that without regulation, compliance and ethics it would be harder for solicitors and law firms to survive in this increasingly diverse and competitive marketplace.

For the purposes of this book, we are using the term regulation to mean the principles, rules and other requirements that govern our processes and behaviour. Solicitors qualified in England and Wales must consider the role of the Solicitors Regulation Authority (SRA) in this context.

The SRA regulates all such solicitors, regardless of where or how they practise, and it is also entitled to authorise law firms to provide reserved legal activities to members of the public. The SRA does this in compliance with the Legal Services Act 2007 and other statutory entitlements, and because it is an approved regulator. It must ensure that its style and policy supports what are described as the 'regulatory objectives' in Section 1 of the Legal Services Act.

Compliance is a responsibility thrust upon individual solicitors, the owners and managers of SRA-authorised law firms, and everyone else working within these firms. In using this term we mean compliance with the previously mentioned principles, rules, requirements and other similar obligations that have been variously created, described and enforced by the SRA.

Ethics (sometimes also described as professional ethics, legal ethics or professional conduct) describes the entry point standards of behaviour within the profession.

These standards incorporate how we are expected to behave toward our clients, the court, each other and indeed the public at large.

The source material to help with our understanding of these expectations is largely contained in the SRA Standards and Regulations (the 'STaRs'), whose predecessor was the SRA Handbook:

The standards and requirements we expect our regulated community to achieve and observe, for the benefit of the clients they serve and in the public interest.[1]

No one with an interest in these law firm topics can acquire the requisite knowledge without knowing the content of the STaRs.

The STaRs were launched in November 2019, replacing the SRA Handbook, and are in a somewhat different style. Commenting in June 2018, Paul Philip, SRA chief executive, said as follows:

We are now ready to make the changes that are needed to modernise both our regulation and the legal market. Our reforms focus on what matters: the high professional standards that offer real public protection rather than unnecessary bureaucracy that generates costs, constrains firms and hinders access to legal services. We believe that the changes will make it easier for firms and solicitors to do business and to meet the needs of those who need their services.[2]

We have added commentary about these changes in the narrative of this book, and the SRA's table of changes in Section 4.

Regulation, compliance and ethics link and overlap. The loss of one of these components from an individual's or law firm's ways of working makes survival or longevity more difficult to achieve.

The following truths must therefore be acknowledged and evidenced:

- Regulation maintains the standing of the legal profession and we are all answerable to a regulatory body, the SRA.
- Compliance with regulatory standards must be in evidence; we must be able to prove that we are complying with these regulatory requirements.
- Professional ethics must be part of individual and firm-wide decision-making.
- All of the above must reflect current requirements as imposed variously by the regulator, other external forces and our client base and on the basis that this is a dynamic topic.

Finally, thinking about regulation, compliance and ethics means that there must be an assessment of risk – of breach or failure to comply – and how to manage it. For these purposes risk management denotes the identification of possible risk events and the measures that are implemented to identify and mitigate these risks.

This book is intended to assist busy practitioners with essential knowledge about these topics. It is a reference manual for anyone needing to satisfy themselves that they can demonstrate accountability and that their responses to regulation, compliance and ethics will withstand scrutiny.

The core subjects are divided into four sections:
- Governance and risk management
- Regulatory compliance
- Legal compliance
- Compliance in practice (tools and resources)

In each section, the key topics are discussed with an explanation of essential knowledge and suggestions for practical solutions. The knowledge narrative draws on regulatory expectations, ethical behaviours and various cases and SRA disciplinary findings to demonstrate why particular subjects are relevant and what are the consequences of misunderstandings. Commentary on disciplinary decisions is drawn from the public record. The practical solutions include compliance strategies, top tips, checklists and tables, and contributions from various thought leaders adding their own perspective and experience to the discussions.

Regulation, compliance and ethics matter! It is essential that firms understand what is expected of each individual within the entity and have answers to the questions against which they will be tested. Only the correct answers will keep the firm in business.

Section 1: Governance and risk management

Introduction

This book is intended to be a practical companion for busy practitioners.

Regardless of whether you are a compliance professional employed in a law firm to oversee all matters relating to its continuing authorisation, an owner of the business with the motivation of success and profit, or are otherwise employed in or connected with a SRA-authorised law firm, there is a need to understand the importance of regulation, compliance and ethics.

An understanding is offered as to the importance of regulation, the ability to achieve and demonstrate regulatory and legal compliance to various stakeholders, and the capacity to create an environment in which ethical behaviours have a home.

Compliance will only happen where there is effective law firm management, and a firm will be well managed if there is a commitment to the three core concepts explored in this section.

First, the SRA (principally, but joined in some circumstances by other interested stakeholders) expects law firms to be run and managed in much the same way as other commercial enterprises. This interest in our business acumen may be a surprise, but for regulatory reasons described in this chapter we must engage with this stated interest of the SRA.

Secondly, and to be frank, our legal education is often inadequate when it comes to developing the necessary business acumen. Many firms might find that they need to facilitate this learning, and to consider not only pure business and financial skills but also skills relating to client and people management.

Thirdly, in addition to these business skills we need to throw into the recipe the extra ingredient of an ethical foundation layer.

This is a big undertaking, but without an understanding of these expectations, individuals and law firms can find themselves under regulatory censure.

In other words, the law firm of the twenty-first century requires so much more than the ability to hire and retain a posse of good lawyers. These lawyers – and indeed everyone else working in the firm and therefore also subject to SRA authorisation – need the support that comes from working in a well-run law firm with an ethical core.

In this section, we will look at what this means in practice. We will examine the meaning of risk management, what this requires from everyone in the business, and the role of effective supervision in the workplace. Specialist thought leaders contribute to the narrative to add their perspective and to help with informed decision-making.

Chapter 1: Effective law firm management

Introduction

Back in the day, how a law firm was managed was not of huge relevance to the regulatory body overseeing the profession. This meant that compliance was a backroom function (if, in fact, a function at all). It was good enough for a firm to hire technically competent individuals and to see that they delivered legal services that did not attract complaint.

In fact, complaints from clients were one of the biggest motivatory forces pushing forwards regulatory policy and disciplinary work. In terms of the relationship between solicitors and law firms and the regulatory body (which was the Law Society of England and Wales until 2007), fewer complaints meant less need to have regulatory conversations. Moving forward to modern times, to be precise the period since the introduction of the Legal Services Act 2007 and the establishment of the SRA, this is not sufficient.

We are now working in an environment where legal services regulators must be approved and ensure that their work supports the regulatory objectives of the Act. They are overseen by the Legal Services Board and must demonstrate compliance with the Legal Services Act.

The SRA is the approved regulator of solicitors and this status means that it is able to authorise law firms in England and Wales. Whilst complaints can

> "In regulatory thinking, any notion of a honeymoon period, in terms of understanding the SRA and its objectives, is a distant memory and we are expected to understand the significance of regulation, compliance and ethics."

of course still trigger regulatory scrutiny, this is not the only or main driving force. There is also the need to prove to the regulator that you, as an individual or as a law firm, are a safe provider of legal services based on the regulator's risk analysis of what jeopardises the delivery of these services.

It is not uncommon for this change of tone and emphasis to be misunderstood in the workplace. There are several reasons for this. The change may not have been on the radar of those lawyers who have worked in the profession for a number of years, many of whom remain of the belief that there is little need to be accountable to the regulator, taking the view that their relationship with the regulator is a long distance one which focuses on the issue of practising certificates only. This is not so; the SRA is entitled to satisfy itself that the decisions it makes to authorise people and law firms are not detrimental. New entrants to the profession are reliant on the providers of their vocational training courses to bring this to their attention. Sadly, for a number of reasons, gaining this knowledge is sometimes hit and miss.

However, in regulatory thinking, any notion of a honeymoon period, in terms of understanding the SRA and its objectives, is a distant memory and we are expected to understand the significance of regulation, compliance and ethics. Developing a good working relationship with the regulator, understanding the legal and regulatory non-negotiables, and ensuring that colleagues are ethically minded are part of the essential mix that we are expected to achieve in practice. Compliance, in all its different variations, is a central function of the modern law firm.

The evidence that this must be the case is encapsulated in the SRA Principles. By way of reminder, the Principles are at the heart of the SRA's regulatory toolkit. The SRA describes them in this way:

The SRA Principles comprise the fundamental tenets of ethical behaviour that we expect all those we regulate to uphold.

The Principles set both the scene and the tone for the relationship with the regulator and for the provision of legal services. They apply to solicitors and everyone else working in SRA-authorised firms. Breach can have consequences for the individual concerned and also for the firm in which they are working.

To illustrate this point, let's consider the repercussions for individual and firm in the following matter.

Case study

In 2017, the Solicitors Disciplinary Tribunal[3] ordered that an SRA-authorised law firm, Locke Lord (UK) LLP, pay a fine of £500,000. It was found that the firm had failed to prevent one of its employees from involving himself in, holding out the firm as being involved in, and using the firm's client account in transactions that bore the hallmarks of dubious financial arrangements or investment schemes. This was held to be in breach of the SRA Principles concerned with integrity, acting in clients' best interests, trust in the profession and proper governance.

The employee was a solicitor and a partner in the firm and his behaviour was also referred to the Solicitors Disciplinary Tribunal (SDT). Seven allegations were upheld against the individual; it was found that he had not undertaken due diligence on behalf of clients and had misled third parties, failed to protect client money and acted in conflict of interest situations. He has been struck off the roll of solicitors.

Knowing your starting point

The regulatory objectives in the Legal Services Act include the approved regulator's role in protecting and promoting the interests of consumers, and this is more likely to be undermined where legal services are provided by law firms that are failing in terms of regulatory compliance and, to be frank, commercially.

- Regardless of your role in the business – whether you are an owner of the business, a lawyer, member of support staff or one of the myriad other professionals now employed in a law firm – you have a part to play in complying with the Principles (and for that matter, all other relevant parts of the Standards and Regulations) and the duties apply to you individually and, in respect of the firm's continuing authorisation, collectively. The secret to compliance is to understand your specific role.

- If you are an owner or manager ('manager' being the SRA's term for a partner, director, member of an LLP or sole practitioner), or otherwise in a senior, decision-making role, then you must ensure that the expectations and requirements you have of colleagues are agreed collectively and that these behaviours are transparent and clearly communicated to them.
- The governance structure of the firm must be agreed and clearly disseminated to everyone in the firm.
- You must be clear about the risks that are present in your type of law firm and you must have strategies to manage and mitigate these risks. The SRA does not provide templates, or pre-judge risks in different firms. We are asked to consider our peculiar circumstances and make judgement calls. What are the worst things that could happen in your firm and what are you doing to try to prevent a risk event occurring?
- The firm must be well managed from the perspective of financial stability. A good lawyer in a financially unsound firm is unlikely to be able to deliver legal services without some constraints. A good lawyer in a firm that closes suddenly and without notice because of financial difficulties is not going to be able to complete legal services for their clients. What is Plan B? What checks and balances are required to ensure that financial events are not a surprise?

In other words, there must be a risk-based approach to regulation, compliance and ethics that must be understood by everyone in the firm. The firm's continuing authorisation (and, as a by-product, the firm's continuing commercial success and positive reputational profile) is every individual's responsibility. The firm is only as safe as its weakest link and that could be anybody.

This is relatively new, but not so new a concept that we are given the benefit of the doubt. The SRA's regulatory motivator, and therefore a requirement in terms of the management strategy and focus, must be understood.

Disciplinary decisions always make these points more forcefully than a narrative describing the regulatory reference. Turning again to the SDT decision on Locke Lord (UK) LLP, the commentary in the judgment described the firm's omissions in respect of their employee, the First Respondent, in the following terms, by saying the firm had

- *failed to prevent the First Respondent from involving himself (and holding out the Firm as being involved in) and using the Firm's client account in transactions that bore the hallmarks of dubious financial arrangements or investment schemes ...;*
- *failed to prevent the First Respondent from directing or requesting payments into, and transfers or withdrawals from, the Firm's client account ...; and*
- *failed to properly supervise the matters.*

In each of these examples, what is suggested is that the consequent outcomes could have been different if there had been effective management in evidence.

This case, and of course many other similar examples of investigations and rulings by the SDT, illustrates the importance of the following:

- understanding the meaning of effective governance, both from the SRA's perspective and in practice in our businesses;
- knowing what the SRA expects from us;
- acknowledging and building the components of a proper governance response; and
- identifying the role-holders and key strategies that will bind this all together.

The end result will be a law business that holds no surprises for the

SRA. Indeed, a law firm that is of relatively low interest to the regulator with its risk-based agenda is a business that has a compliance and ethical core, and one that attracts and retains clients through its business methods and overarching culture.

SRA risk management expectations
The SRA is an approved regulator that has adopted a style of regulatory response known as risk-based regulation. This means it has much in common with numerous other regulatory bodies, both in the United Kingdom and overseas, who have all in recent times adopted this means of ensuring protection for those seeking and receiving services provided by those individuals and entities they are required to oversee.

We see risk-based regulation not only in the legal services sector but also in such areas as financial services, environmental protection and health, safety and/or food hygiene, to name but a few. It is a common response to consumer-based needs and it should not be a surprise to find this style in our own profession.

This recent trend has its roots in a common theme: what are the best ways to ensure that risks to the public are managed and mitigated? How do we keep safe standards at the forefront of how services are provided? How can the public retain confidence in the services that they receive?

Of course, there are hidden depths to these seemingly straightforward questions, particularly when firms are expected to demonstrate their responses. To offer a few examples as to what lies behind this theme:
- How are risks analysed?
- Why does the regulator prioritise some risks and not others?
- Who influences the regulator's priority calls?

The SRA explains its position, and more importantly its expectations of us, on its website. It makes, for example, the following statement:
Risk-based regulation means that risks to us acting compatibly with the regulatory objectives are assessed in terms of their probability and

17

the impact of any harm they cause to desired outcomes, before action is taken. This approach ensures that regulatory activities and resources are prioritised and applied proportionately.[4]

The SRA determines risk – if we can assume that this means the likelihood of an adverse incident or event happening at some point in the future – by linking it to some core reference points:

- Does the risk that has been identified have an impact on the SRA's overarching regulatory duty, which is to ensure that the regulatory objectives are put into practice?
- Does the identified risk have the potential to damage the reputation of the solicitor brand?
- Does the identified risk have the potential to have adverse consequences for law firm clients, or more generally consumers seeking legal services from solicitors and authorised law firms?

These reference points trigger the need for a regulatory response from us, both in an individual capacity, if we are either solicitors or non-solicitors employed in an SRA-authorised law firm, and in terms of law firm management overall. Risk-based regulation requires us to understand what risks matter to the regulator and to consider and prioritise the same within the firm and, more widely, to have a systematic response to the management and mitigation of all risks within the firm.

This should not be interpreted as meaning that the SRA requires, or even imagines, that law firms will be risk-free zones. This would be an unrealistic ambition on the part of both the regulator and the regulated. Instead, it is a regulatory duty presented to us in terms of needing to control the likelihood and impact of risk events through effective law firm management.

A further consequence of this style of regulation is for both the regulator and the regulated to be open, transparent and communicative. The SRA does not expect us to second guess what its priorities might be and equally it does not expect us to hide risk events from it. Again, there will be some individuals within your law firm for whom this is a surprise.

This is a (fairly) new-style regulatory relationship with which some colleagues may be unfamiliar, and they may be wary of being transparent. This is a considerable challenge for many owners, managers and compliance professionals who must find the right language to convince colleagues that individual openness and accountability is expected of them.

The SRA's risk priorities
There are two main features to the thinking behind SRA's risk prioritisation. First, this is thinking out loud so that we know exactly what concerns the regulator; and secondly, prioritisation is fluid and dynamic. Regulatory risk thinking is constantly evolving.

This has consequences for us in respect of our risk response; we are expected to know what the SRA thinks, we must keep up to date with their ever-changing thoughts and we are expected to produce risk responses that are appropriate.

The SRA Risk Outlook provides us with the primary source material for our risk responses. This is an annual publication, described on the SRA website as follows:[5]

The Outlook sets out what we think are the key risks and challenges faced by the profession. By sharing our views, and what we think can be done to address the issues, we hope to help you get to grips with the challenges. The impact on the users of legal services when things go wrong can be devastating and we all want to avoid that.[6]

It is a regulatory guide designed to ensure that there is a common starting point for the risk discussions and deliberations in which we must engage.

The Outlook supports the contention that the regulator is dynamic; it has been republished annually since 2013, with seasonal updates along the way. The table below gives an indication of the priorities over this period.

Table 1 below invites some interesting questions and observations:
- Why have some risks (for example, protection of client money and money laundering) been a constant feature of consecutive Outlooks? This can be answered by considering the severity of

their impact; these are deal-breakers in terms of the regulatory objectives or because of the detriment that is caused to the solicitor brand and/or to clients.

By way of example, think of the trust the public places in us to protect their money and think of the consequences of any loss for whatever reason.

Such is the importance of this duty, we have a number of disciplinary decisions providing evidence that we cannot compromise ourselves and provide inadequate protections. The following examples illustrate this point, and are also used to stress that the amount of money is rarely taken into account when breaches of regulatory requirements are considered.

Case study

Consider the SDT ruling against Christopher Howdle,[7] a solicitor who had "harmed public confidence in the profession" by failing to safeguard client money. The SDT found that he had made improper transfers from client accounts to a value of approximately £2 million.

The findings included the following commentary:

The Respondent had held client money and this placed him in a position of trust. He had acted in breach of that position of trust ... The Respondent's misconduct had harmed public confidence in the profession. The public would expect a solicitor who was holding their money to safeguard their money and only use it for their matter.

The tribunal also added:

Client account should be sacrosanct, and every solicitor should know that it is to be treated as sacrosanct. The respondent had made numerous improper payments from client account, and that made his misconduct particularly serious.

Mr Howden was struck off the roll of solicitors and ordered to pay costs of £27,000.

Table 1: Risk priorities identified by the SRA in Risk Outlooks published since 2015

2015/16	2016/17	2017/18	2018/19	2019/20
Failure to provide a proper standard of service, particularly for vulnerable people	Standards of service and consideration of vulnerability	Lack of access to legal services	Access to legal services	Anti-money laundering
Misuse of client money	Information security	Standards of service	Cyber security	Client money
Lack of a diverse and representative profession	Independence and integrity	Investment schemes	Diversity in the profession	Diversity in the profession
Lack of independence	Protecting client money	Information security	Information security	Information and cyber security
Failure to act with integrity: improper or abusive litigation	Money laundering	Protecting client money	Integrity and ethics	Integrity and ethics
Information security and cyber-crime	Diversity	Money laundering	Investment schemes	Investment schemes
Bogus law firms		Independence and integrity	Managing claims	Managing claims
Money laundering – inadequate systems and control over the transfer of money		Diversity in the profession	Protecting client money	Meeting legal needs
			Standards of service	Standards of service

In another decision, the sanction was similar – the solicitor concerned was also removed from the roll and made to pay costs of £21,000. The SDT finding against Mr Vernon Burke was triggered by what Mr Burke had described as a "tidying-up" exercise of historic client account balances.[8] We are told that Mr Burke had "cleared off residual balances on client accounts to a total value of £3,826 by issuing bills of costs and paying them from client funds when there was no proper justification to do so and without first sending those bills or other written notifications of the costs to the relevant clients".

The SDT finding was that a "solicitor of integrity did not clear off residual balances, however small, without first taking steps to be absolutely certain he was entitled to the money" and his behaviour showed "lack of moral soundness, a lack of rectitude and no adherence to an ethical code".

- Some risks retain high priority status because of the interest external stakeholders have in the subject and in the profession. For example, money laundering (or, more accurately, our role in anti-money laundering programmes) is subject to government and international control. The SRA must monitor us to ensure our response is appropriate and that we play our part as gatekeepers in deterrence programmes. This duty is explored in more detail in Section 3 of this book. For the time being, consider the disciplinary consequences of failings in this area.

Case study

In an SDT matter, which upheld a regulatory settlement agreement made with the SRA, the actions of the firm of Clyde & Co LLP and three of the firm's partners were considered.[9] The respondents, both the firm and the partners, were found to have used the client account as a banking facility, thereby acting in breach of the relevant SRA Principles, SRA Code and the SRA Accounts Rules, and not to have complied with their obligations under the Money Laundering Regulations.

Whilst there was no suggestion that there had been any lack of integrity, probity or trustworthiness on the part of any of the respondents, the firm was fined £50,000 and each of the partners was fined £10,000. The SDT commentary included the following:

> *Each of the Respondents has let down the profession and their actions would tend to diminish rather than maintain the trust the public would place in them and in the provision of legal services. The defaults in question were particularly glaring as the Firm was a large and, previously, reputable firm; it would be expected to set an example to other firms in its compliance systems.*

- Some risks are included because of external factors that might undermine our core values. For example, information security is now prioritised both because of the developments in cyber criminology and because of the severity of data protection legislation, which need to be managed alongside the need to be able to be viewed as trustworthy custodians of personal data from the client perspective. Interestingly, the SRA Handbook that came into force in 2011 includes no reference to cyber-crime, and neither do the current STaRs, yet many of the SRA's risk resources are designed to educate us about the risks and what we are expected to do to manage the risks in our workplaces and to protect our clients' interests. For example, the SRA published a downloadable resource in December 2016 called "IT Security: Keeping information and money safe"[10] and regularly uses its website to highlight identity frauds and other cyber-crimes. In return for collating and publishing this information, we are expected to keep informed about the risks.

Section 1: Governance and risk management

Table 2: Risk management considerations

Risk priority	Management considerations
Meeting legal needs	Are there practices we could deploy to increase the range of services we could offer and thereby improve consumer choice?
Standards of service	Are we confident that our communication skills are suited to the needs of all our clients? Do we need to develop bespoke responses for particular types of client? Do our people need training to identify when it is appropriate to adapt the standard response?
Investment schemes	Have we considered the SRA's warning notice on these topics? Do we know our clients sufficiently well? Are we sufficiently robust about the use of client account? Is training necessary?
Information and cyber security	Are we sufficiently cyber aware? Do we consider risks to information security from all our different ways of holding information? Are our premises secure? Do we have an understandable internal reporting system that addresses all the variations of the risks?
Client money	Are we confident that all relevant staff have had appropriate training on the risks of handling client money? Do we supervise this aspect of our business adequately? Do we trust but vet our account signatories? Do we consider cyber-based risks?
Anti-money laundering	Is our training and risk awareness response appropriate and up to date? Are colleagues taking responsibility for risk awareness and reporting? Do our file reviews and auditing systems incorporate oversight of this risk?
Integrity and ethics	Do we circulate the SRA's risk resources to staff? Do we empower our colleagues to understand and deliver ethical behaviour? Are we confident that we work with ethical colleagues? Are we managing the internal and external pressures that may contribute to failures to act with independence and/or integrity?
Diversity in the profession	Are we creating an inclusive culture in the workplace? Do we monitor our diversity statistics? Do we screen policies, systems etc to ensure fairness?
Managing claims	Are we confident that the claims we pursue are legitimate and we are not breaching our duties to uphold the rule of law and the proper administration of justice? Do we deliver the right messages to our staff about the checks they must make of clients and claims? Are we challenging inappropriate behaviour from clients and colleagues etc? Have we considered the SRA's 2017 warning notice on holiday sickness claims?[11]

Table 1, and the concept of risk-based regulation more generally, also triggers the following questions within the workplace:
- Would the SRA be satisfied with our response to risk-based regulation?
- How do we ensure that we understand current regulatory risk thinking?
- Do we have the right systems and process responses to risk analysis?
- How do we instil ownership of risk management in every individual working within the firm?

Many of the solutions to these questions become easier to identify and demonstrate through proper governance. Table 2, above, offers possible solutions to the risk management questions that arise in respect of the current risk priorities.

Compliance strategies – demonstrating effective governance

'Effective governance' is a phrase that is used in the STaRs and it is at the heart of any effective risk-based management formula. However, the SRA chooses not to define it. This is deliberate. It means the responsibility for determining what is required is given to those individuals who are better equipped to deliver effective solutions based on their knowledge of their own business – the owners and managers – although we are given clues in the SRA Code of Conduct for Firms; these help with our understanding of risk management considerations.

This is the section of the SRA's regulatory toolkit that sets out the ethical and compliance outcomes we are all required to achieve if we are solicitors and/or working in SRA-authorised law firms. Chapter 2 of the SRA Code of Conduct for Firms contains management standards and assists with an interpretation of how the Principles apply in the context of the management of the law business.

These standards will apply in all contexts and to all law firms and they are shown in the table below.

Table 3: SRA code of conduct for firms, chapter 2: Compliance and Business Systems

Standard	What should we be achieving?
2.1 You have effective governance structures, arrangements, systems and controls in place that ensure: (a) you comply with all the SRA's regulatory arrangements, as well as with other regulatory and legislative requirements, which apply to you; (b) your managers and employees comply with the SRA's regulatory arrangements which apply to them; (c) your managers and interest holders and those you employ or contract with do not cause or substantially contribute to a breach of the SRA's regulatory arrangements by you or your managers or employees; and (d) your compliance officers are able to discharge their duties [under paragraphs 9.1 and 9.2 below].	Do we identify owners of different risk functions? Would everyone in the firm know who they can talk to in respect of their work and their employment? Can we produce up-to-date documented evidence of this? Have we evidence that we undertake regular benchmarking exercises to ensure that we have SRA Standards and Regulations apply to us? Have we documented processes to support compliance with those parts of the STaRs that apply to us? Do we ensure that our expectations about regulatory compliance are communicated effectively to all colleagues in the firm? Do we give our compliance officers the right tools, resources and powers to ensure that they fulfil their personal duties?
2.2 You keep and maintain records to demonstrate compliance with your obligations under the SRA's regulatory arrangements.	Do we have sufficient evidence to demonstrate that everyone understands their role in maintaining regulatory compliance standards? Do we have records of breaches?
2.3 You remain accountable for compliance with the SRA's regulatory arrangements where your work is carried out through others, including your managers and those you employ or contract with.	Do we convey the right messages to our colleagues and others associated with our business that compliance and adherence to our arrangements, systems and controls is mandatory? Have we evidence that we monitor for this compliance?
2.4 You actively monitor your financial stability and business viability. Once you are aware that you will cease to operate, you effect the orderly wind-down of your activities.	Do we have processes to control budgets, expenditure and cash flow? Do we identify and monitor financial risks?

continued on next page

Chapter 1: Effective law firm management

Standard	What should we be achieving?
2.5 You identify, monitor and manage all material risks to your business, including those which may arise from your connected practices.	Do we proactively consider risks that are present, or could arise, in the business taking into account our people, our clients, the services we provide, delivery channels and external threats? Do we have mitigation processes and do we monitor these for effectiveness?

The reporting lines – who should be doing what to demonstrate proper governance?

It is important to understand that management of the effective governance requirement includes identification of the roles that must be assumed by individuals within the firm.

When working out the objectives that must be achieved, the conversation must start at senior level. The table below gives examples of the questions that should be given house room if this requirement is to be considered appropriately. These are partnership-level questions but the answers will require the input of other colleagues.[12]

Table 4: Governance objectives

Question	Why this needs to be asked	What should be achieved
What do we want as partners (directors, members, principal etc)?	Sometimes partnerships are a disparate group of individuals who do not have an agreed common purpose other than to make a profit. It can be seen why this can happen; partners come and go, firms are created and recreated through mergers and lateral hires etc. However, with the regulatory focus on compliance and with the all-pervasive need to be ethical, it is important to have	Disagreements about the firm's governance are contained in the boardroom. There is clarity and effective communication about the partners' collective vision and expectations. There is an agreed purpose for the business with agreement about how this will be achieved.

continued on next page

Section 1: Governance and risk management

Question	Why this needs to be asked	What should be achieved
	the assurances that partners are in agreement about the parameters of the business and where it is heading.	
What do we want to achieve in terms of risk management?	Without evidence that risks are discussed, the relationship with the regulator and others may be more complicated. It is important that the partners agree about the risks that are present and have strategies such as systems, policies and other controls to manage and mitigate those risks.	There is evidence that the partners have discussed risk events and agreed risk priorities. There is an awareness that risk diagnosis is fluid so that risk monitoring is diarised and kept up to date. Both external and internal factors are considered when monitoring. The risk analysis translates into systems and controls designed to minimise the occurrence and/or impact of the risk event. Communication of the requirements is effective and monitoring provides information about success of the strategy, the existence of resistance by individuals to the system, etc.
How will we ensure that proper governance extends to financial controls?	The regulator is concerned about a firm's financial health as this may have consequences in terms of compliance and ethical standards. Do all partners have an understanding of the firm's financial commitments, strategy, high-risk commercial decisions etc?	There are financial risk management processes. The right information is shared with the partners and other relevant parties.
Who will be responsible for what?	Proper governance requires the identification of roles and the allocation of these roles to the right people. What is needed will ultimately depend on the firm's internal	All necessary and/or otherwise appropriate roles have been identified and filled. The role-holders have the right skills to fulfil these roles

continued on next page

Chapter 1: Effective law firm management

Question	Why this needs to be asked	What should be achieved
	composition, its size and even its type of work and workforce. As a minimum, SRA-authorised law firms must have a compliance officer for legal practice and a compliance officer for finance and administration. They also must consider whether they need to have a nominated officer (the money laundering reporting officer) and/or an insurance distribution officer and/or a data protection officer. Other titled roles include heads of department, supervisors, complaints handlers, individuals responsible for indemnity issues, training supervisors, Lexcel and other accreditation scheme lead individuals etc. The individual role-holders should have the right skills, experience and resources to meet the challenges. In the absence of this support for the role-holders, the inference will be that the firm is paying no more than lip service to the regulatory and compliance requirements.	and they are offered ongoing training and other support to ensure that they remain effective. There is transparency about the roles so that everyone from new joiners upwards understands the reporting lines. The reporting lines are part of a network of regulatory and compliance intelligence such as is necessary to ensure that the firm fulfils its responsibilities to manage risks and work with its regulator and other interested stakeholders.
What systems and controls do we need to construct?	The regulator expects a demonstration of accountability. Systems and processes provide the evidence that there is proper governance.	The systems and controls accurately reflect what is needed in the circumstances. They are not off-the-shelf solutions but tailored to the firm and take into account size, location, composition, work streams etc. There is monitoring of suitability of the systems and their application by colleagues.

continued on next page

29

Question	Why this needs to be asked	What should be achieved
		The requirement to comply with the systems is clear to all colleagues. Records are kept and used to address any breaches or other issues such as training needs or disciplinary action.
What messages do we want to deliver in respect of our compliance culture and ethics?	The partners agree the culture of the business in respect of the legal and regulatory compliance obligations and the ethical persuasion.	The compliance and ethical atmosphere is not obscure but visible for all to see. The partners set the tone for the expected responses. There is clarity about the importance of this, with training given as necessary, and assistance available to support the right compliance and ethical choices.

Strategies: Bringing role-holders into the governance structure

Creating a proper governance structure will be evidenced by people charts, organograms and the like. These can be beautifully crafted documents but will be meaningless, and reviewed critically by the SRA, unless named role-holders understand, firstly, that they are included and, secondly, what expectations lie behind their titles.

In other words, if effective risk management requires proper governance, proper governance in turn needs to be supported by individuals who have specific roles and clearly described responsibilities and reporting duties. Consider the following roles and expectations.

The partners' role

The vanguard of the governance movement must be the firm's partnership and we have already suggested some of the questions that they should be asking and that will shape the firm's response to governance requirements.

There are stumbling blocks along the way and it is not uncommon to find that in some firms, partners still do not understand the importance of being one collective voice in terms of the response to regulation, compliance and ethics. Such unity is essential. Anything other than this position, and the firm's regulatory journey is on a rockier road.

The one-voice anthem has to start at the top, with the individuals who have most to lose if the business flounders. This means that the partners are at the top of the risk management pyramid and they must be in agreement about what they collectively want to achieve. In order for the seriousness of these topics and the collective response to be communicated in as clear and transparent a way as possible, there must be no scope for variation or deviation in terms of the response to the firm's management systems etc. This consistency will not be achieved unless the partners are in agreement about their regulatory and ethical goals and how these will be achieved in practice through effective compliance strategies.

This is easier said than done. Lawyers are not always comfortable with being team players but there must be shared values and common speak about certain topics. The table below shows the areas in which there ought to be a consensual approach from the partners.

Table 5: Partners' consensual approach

Topic	Justification of the need for consensus	What needs to be agreed?
Integrity	Some would argue that acting with integrity is what distinguishes a lawyer (and by implication, all those working in law firms) from other business people. They would be right. SRA Principle 5 states that "you act with integrity" with the guidance that whilst someone acting dishonestly can be said to be acting without integrity, the concept of integrity is wider than just acting dishonestly.	How do we explain the meaning of integrity in our firm? Where will we express this value? What messages will we give our colleagues on our expectations about integrity in their work? How will we help colleagues who might feel that their personal integrity is being jeopardised (for example, less experienced colleagues who are

continued on next page

Section 1: Governance and risk management

Topic	Justification of the need for consensus	What needs to be agreed?
	The SRA chooses not to define the concept any further, but it frequently judges individuals against this Principle. Solicitors found to have failed to demonstrate integrity face severe disciplinary consequences including referral to the SDT and removal from the roll. Non-solicitors have also had orders made against them preventing their employment in SRA-authorised firms. Lord Jackson offered some insights in a 2018 appeal case by discussing what is meant by lack of integrity.[13] He said integrity was "a useful shorthand to express the higher standards which society expects from professional persons and which the professions expect from their own members". Lack of integrity more broadly can have reputational and commercial consequences for the individual and their employer.	being pressured into acting incorrectly, perhaps by other colleagues or by clients etc)? How do we monitor individuals' adherence to our expectations? What will be the consequence if we identify that an individual has acted without integrity?
Decisions about how the correct regulatory, compliance and ethical responses will be facilitated and evidenced	Without evidence of what you are doing, there is a risk that no one – not least the regulator, your professional indemnity insurer and your clients – will believe you and what you say that you have done or not done. Being able to demonstrate accountability is an investment in a less stressful relationship with your stakeholders. At the very least this means that the firm must appoint compliance officers (a	The compliance officer positions should be filled by the most appropriate individuals. The compliance officers should have sufficient resources to ensure that they are able to keep themselves and the firm safe from scrutiny. If the compliance officers are also fee earners, there should be due consideration by both the role-holders and the partnership about the impact that the compliance role will

continued on next page

Chapter 1: Effective law firm management

Topic	Justification of the need for consensus	What needs to be agreed?
	compulsory regulatory requirement). These roles are analysed in more detail below. For now, it is important to understand that the role-holders must have the support of the business owners and have the facilities and resources to fulfil their duties. More consideration may be needed to support the compliance officers. This will largely depend on the partners' analysis about the presence of risk in their environment. In some firms, there are compliance teams (including specialists considering the regulatory and ethical decisions that are needed in respect of conflicts of interests, confidentiality/disclosure duties, anti-money laundering matters etc). In other firms, this is not considered necessary but the fee earners are expected to be responsible for risk management. Accountability also requires commitment to systems and processes. Consistency is an effective deterrent to risk. Having systems that are compulsory is a way of managing risk, a means to produce evidence of the risk response and a way of highlighting risk events and other regulatory and ethical breach matters.	have on their fee-earning expectations. Do we have documented proof that we are doing what we say? Is it understood that everyone has a role to play in managing and monitoring risk and that this extends to reporting/self-reporting concerns and mistakes etc? Are the consequences of a breach of systems etc clear? Do colleagues understand that they must accept that decisions may be made which they may not agree with (for example, a prospective client not being incepted because of risk evaluations) but which they nevertheless must accept?

continued on next page

Section 1: Governance and risk management

Topic	Justification of the need for consensus	What needs to be agreed?
Decisions about the interplay between regulatory, compliance and ethical duties and the commercial aspects of running a law firm	Of course, the partners will have a vested interest in ensuring the longevity of their business. This means that the business must make a profit and be commercially orientated. Conversely, the business will be short-lived if regulatory and ethical considerations are not factored into decisions and any risks discussed, evaluated and managed.	Do we agree on the regulatory and ethical framework within which we will operate? Have we made it clear to all colleagues that there are some decisions that may make sense to them from a commercial viewpoint, but which place us in an invidious position with the SRA, and that we will not adopt the riskier approach?
Focusing on client care standards	Regulatory purpose is largely focused on client protection. SRA Principle 7 requires us to act in a client's best interests. Breach of this principle can trigger regulatory action against the individual and the firm. Additionally, there is the need to consider the role of the Office of Legal Complaints (LeO).	Do we agree on what services we will provide and what we will not? Do we agree about the resources we will make available so that services can be delivered safely? Is it clear what we expect of fee earners and the role that support staff have in the business? Have we communicated our expectations about the internal systems and processes that are mandatory? Do we have the means to monitor for compliance?
Response to bad behaviour	Sadly, every firm has its miscreants. These might be good mavericks; for example, those who bring in clients and generate healthy earnings but do not wish to be distracted by systems and controls. Maybe they are lateral hires who bring with them different habits and routines that are not in harmony with your firm's requirements. Or they	Does the partnership have an agreed and unanimous response to bad behaviour? Has the partnership agreed its tolerance levels and have these been communicated to the rest of the firm? Is there agreement about how the firm will deal with the mavericks? Is support given to other employees who may feel

continued on next page

Chapter 1: Effective law firm management

Topic	Justification of the need for consensus	What needs to be agreed?
	might be bad mavericks; the individuals who sometimes seem simply unmanageable. Both types of rebel are a risk to the firm's regulatory status and reputation. They consequently pose a threat to the partners and compliance officers who are in the regulatory spotlight if questions are asked about how the firm manages risks.	pressured by the maverick individual?
Understanding and agreeing on financial management strategies	Some partners will be more inclined to take financial risks and undertake new financial ventures than others. Individuals will have different expectations/ requirements about profit levels, the need for drawings, and profit-sharing agreements. SRA regulation is concerned about our financial management strategies. The clues are in the SRA Standards and Regulations, particularly with the standards relating to effective governance in chapter 2 of the SRA Code of conduct for Firms.	Is there an agreed management plan/strategy that incorporates future financial planning topics? Do we keep our financial planning under review? Do we have the capacity to adapt financial strategies to accommodate changed circumstances? Do all partners agree about the need for drawings/profit sharing/future expenditure to correlate with the accurate financial position?

AN INSIDER'S INSIGHT

Alexander Pelopidas is a partner at London law firm Rosling King LLP. Here are his thoughts on the topic:

Q: What do you see as the risks that arise when the partnership is not in agreement about the firm's ethical and compliance position?

As I see it, there are two main risks that a lack of agreement or 'buy-in' would create. Firstly, the likely variation in approach will cause confusion for staff who won't have a clear message as to what their roles are in ensuring the firm is compliant and safe. Secondly, at the extreme end, it presents opportunities for exploitation not only from those externally who would seek to gain advantage but also those internally (if any) that may be able to operate under the radar in the confusion.

Q: How do you ensure that your partners are committed to an ethical way of business?

The way a firm does business should permeate everything it does from its marketing and client services to its internal management. It's not only about messages and policies outlining the firm's ethos, it's about involving all partners to build those messages and policies so they believe them too; as ultimately, a law firm is built on its people.

Q: As a partner, what behaviours do you insist on from your colleagues?

I expect my fellow partners to buy into policies and approaches we agree on, to be open and alive to change in all aspects of running a firm and willing to share responsibilities.

Q: What are your tips for introducing effective compliance measures into the workplace?

More planning goes into implementing new compliance measures than people might appreciate at first. In addition to drafting and agreeing new policies and training, systems and processes may need to be reviewed and new ones put in place. Often working out what needs to be implemented in terms of your business is the first and hardest step. The new anti-money laundering (AML) and GDPR regulations reflected this for my firm. I would recommend taking time as early as possible to work out what you need to do rather than rush into anything, only to later find out it was unnecessary or you missed something. In terms of training on the new measures, I have found that often staff will be far more receptive to training provided by an external provider. And finally, keep everything under review; new guidance on compliance always comes out that may require you to tweak elements of your new policies.

The role of the management team
Some firms will be of the type and size where involving the whole body of partners in decision-making is too cumbersome. In these cases it is logical that decision-making about regulation, compliance, ethics and risk management strategies should be devolved, and responsibilities carved up into smaller groups.

It is not uncommon in larger businesses for the management role to be delivered by a management team and for there to be role-holders with titles such as managing partner, chief executive, head of practice, chief finance officer and similar, being part of what can be described as the executive committee. In many modern firms, some of the role-holders are not solicitors themselves but have been brought in to add their business and commercial expertise. This is usually a positive addition to the dynamics of a law firm in competition with many other similar businesses. However, these non-solicitors must understand the restrictions and duties of working in an SRA-authorised business and in a regulated industry.

Whatever its title, this group will coordinate the firm's management response, ensuring that the firm is fulfilling its regulatory duties as well as operating on a sensible, comfortable commercial footing.

If this is your solution to law firm management, then the essential considerations are as follows:
- Do we have the right people in the team? Suggestions would include a membership group comprising a managing partner, the head of finance/practice manager, the compliance officers, the quality and risk leaders, head of human resources and those with senior roles in business strategy and marketing.
- Does the team have the right membership to make it an effective operational unit?
- Do we have a clearly agreed role? By which we mean the following: Does the team have an agreed and understood remit that includes the steerage of the risk management of the firm?
- Does the team have the right structure in terms of team roles such as chair, secretary etc?
- Do we have evidence of our decision-making? If assembled correctly, the management team plays a crucial role in the way in which the firm develops. Is this documented?
- How do we report to the partners? Accountability is crucial so there must be the means to ensure that there are reporting lines to and from the partners, who will want to be in a position of overall endorsement of management team decisions.
- How do we ensure that decisions made by the management team, and approved by the partners, are communicated in an appropriate way to the right colleagues? The management team is demonstrating compliance in practice. This requires effective communication. Will there be a liaison mechanism between the team and ambassadors from different departments or different locations? Alternatively, will management decisions be communicated via intranet, team or office meetings etc?

Legal counsel

As with some other solutions described in this book, the concept of legal counsel (sometimes described as general counsel) is still relatively novel and largely confined to larger, commercially based law firms.

We are of course talking about a lawyer taking the role of in-house legal adviser to the firm. This might be a viable addition to the firm's governance structure, providing the firm with a trusted in-house counsel depending on its size and its risk considerations. If it is a sensible addition in your business, then points to consider will include the following:

- The purpose of the role is to support the firm to stay in business, so there is need to consider the scope of the regulatory and commercial skillsets required of the role-holder.
- The role will include delivering legal advice to the firm in a practical and commercially sensitive way in relation to matters that reduce the risks and provide solutions in terms of services delivered.
- The role must extend to a knowledge of regulatory compliance matters that have a bearing on the firm's ongoing survival. The firm must comply with all relevant features in the SRA Standards and Regulations and all relevant legislation and regulations such as anti-money laundering, anti-bribery and data protection duties.
- The role will include the need to factor professional ethics into any decision-making process. No one should underestimate the regulator's wrath if professional ethics are ignored and legal counsel should factor ethical implications into the advice that they provide to their employer. This requires the role-holder to have knowledge of the relevant sections of the SRA Standards and Regulations together with an understanding of ethics in practice and regulatory decisions based on unethical conduct.
- The role-holder will need to have excellent drafting, negotiation and management skills.
- Advice will need to be delivered to the management team and/or the overarching partnership in a timely and risk-aware manner.
- The role-holder should have a direct reporting line to the owners

of the business. In effect the owners are his or her client and duties are owed to them to act in their best interests.

Heads of department and supervisors

As the titles imply, any individual who is the head of their department (or perhaps a team leader or team head etc), or a supervisor, is in a trusted position where their seniority and loyalty to the firm will be relied upon by the partners as a further component in the governance structure.

In many ways, these role-holders are the lifeblood of the business, providing the connecting links between the partners/management team (of which they might also be part) and the majority of the workforce. Put another way, they are ambassadors for the partnership; their roles are essential if management decisions are to be effective. They also have a role in highlighting people, systems and any other factors that may undermine the partners' expectations.

The job descriptions of these individuals must include this management role. It may be that the role-holders require additional support or training to have confidence to fulfil the business's expectations of them.

The role of effective supervision is crucial – we are not just describing the roles given to certain individuals to supervise the quality of work delivered by their colleagues. There is far more to the terms 'supervisor' and 'supervision', and a solicitor who is also a supervisor has personal regulatory duties to ensure effective supervision. This is discussed in more detail later in this chapter.

Compliance officers

Since 2013, it has been a regulatory requirement for all SRA-authorised law firms, regardless of size or structure, to have approved compliance officers in place. This is a compliance duty contained in the SRA Code of Conduct for Firms and breach is likely to lead to scrutiny of the firm and, except in very unusual and unanticipated circumstances, closure of the firm.

There are two designated roles: the compliance officer for legal practice (COLP) and the compliance officer for finance and administration (COFA). The barebones of the job roles are described below. The essence of the roles is to act as a go-between, smoothing and facilitating the relationship between the firm and the SRA.

The COLP must
- be a lawyer and a manager or employee;
- be sufficiently senior to fulfil the role;
- have their designation approved by the SRA;
- take all reasonable steps to ensure compliance with the terms and conditions of the firm's authorisation, except any obligations under the SRA Accounts Rules;
- take all reasonable steps to ensure compliance with any statutory obligations of the firm, its managers, employees and any other interest holders; and
- ensure that a prompt report is made to the SRA of any facts or matters that they reasonably believe are a serious breach.

The COFA must
- be a manager or employee;
- be sufficiently senior to fulfil the role;
- have their designation approved by the SRA;
- take all reasonable steps to ensure compliance with the terms and conditions of the SRA Accounts Rules; and
- ensure that a prompt report is made to the SRA of any facts or matters that they reasonably believe are a serious breach.

Agreeing to take on either of these roles changes the individual's relationship with the SRA and might have disciplinary consequences.

There are now a number of SDT decisions that have highlighted the personal obligations of the individual role-holder and the consequences of failing to meet the SRA's expectations.

For example, consider the following case in which a firm's non-solicitor practice manager and COFA was rebuked by the SRA in a regulatory settlement agreement in 2016.

Case study

Mr Jonathan Beck was employed in an SRA-authorised law firm, Black Norman Solicitors. The SRA reported, *inter alia*, that the firm had provided a banking facility for two clients between 2010 and 2015 and had received substantial loans from clients over a number of years. In other words, the firm had breached the SRA Accounts Rules 2011.

Mr Beck was aware of the breaches. In mitigation, Mr Beck said he was unclear about the obligation not to allow client account to be used as a banking facility for clients but that he "intended in good faith to carry out his role in the firm effectively in accordance with proper governance and sound financial and risk management principles". He admitted that his actions had fallen short of the standard of conduct expected, but claimed that this was as the result of "misunderstandings and unintended breaches".

It was found that he had permitted the breaches and failed to meet his obligations as a COFA to take all reasonable steps to ensure that the firm and its managers and employees complied with the SRA Accounts Rules. Mr Beck admitted the breaches and was fined £2,000 and rebuked.

Compliance officers are an essential link between the firm and the SRA. The SRA has sought to provide guidance to prospective role-holders to ensure that they understand the importance of this function. For example, in respect of the COFA role the SRA's advice has been to only accept the role if you have an in-depth knowledge of both the SRA Accounts Rules and the firm's current procedures.[14]

The roles of COLP and COFA require an understanding of the following points:
- The role-holder needs technical knowledge to comply with the oversight, recording and reporting functions. There must be an accurate assessment of the individual's starting position and the knowledge that must be acquired.

- The role-holder also needs an understanding of the firm. Are systems and controls appropriately designed rather than off-the-shelf responses?
- There must be an understanding and appreciation of risk-based regulation and risk management techniques. Has the firm accurately identified real risks and identified appropriate ways to manage and mitigate these risks?
- These roles involve ongoing monitoring and vigilance. The COLP's and COFA's roles do not have an end point. Colleagues must be observed to ensure that the mavericks are detected and managed into a safer position; systems and policies must be monitored to ensure that they remain effective risk management measures; and external influences (such as the SRA's regulatory policies, new legislation, economic and commercial pressures etc) must be kept under review to ensure that nothing or no one alters the risk position and that the risk responses continue to be suitable.
- The roles do not stand apart from the partnership role in managing the firm and overseeing risk management. The SRA Code of Conduct for Firms makes this point clear in paragraphs 2.1(d) and 8.1 which describe the responsibilities of the managers and the relationship between them and the compliance officers. In practice, do the role-holders have the right assurances from the partnership that they will support them and head up a consistent response to regulation, compliance and ethical requirements?
- Are the role-holders comfortable with making important decisions about the need to report serious matters to the regulator? Such decisions may not be made with the blessing of the business owners but will nonetheless need to be made. Does the partnership agree to support the role-holders in such situations?
- Are the roles understood by the individuals within the firm? Is there visibility? Are the role-holders the type of people who can deliver the appropriate compliance measures? It should not be a

blame and shame culture where individuals fear the consequences of reporting concerns or mistakes. Rather, compliance works best in an environment where individuals understand that they have nothing to fear if they are communicative; it is this openness and accountability that will create a safe and sustainable environment.
- The preceding point requires, of course, a position built on trust. Do the COLP and COFA instil trust in their colleagues so that intelligence about risk pinch points flows in an open and timely fashion?
- Do the role-holders have the resources to undertake their functions? If they have other roles within the firm does there need to be an understanding or re-evaluation about expectations of what they can do?
- Should there be succession planning? Lack of role-holders is a breach of SRA regulation. Is there merit in appointing non-mandatory deputy compliance officers who can shadow and support the mandatory roles?
- Finally, and very importantly, do the role-holders have the means to demonstrate compliance in practice? This is where documentary evidence is necessary to reassure the SRA and other stakeholders about the firm's governance and management techniques. The form of the evidence will be dictated by the firm's individual circumstances but may include the following:
  - training programmes;
  - job descriptions;
  - office manual policies;
  - effective supervision and monitoring;
  - a risk register;
  - internal reporting mechanisms;
  - breach logs;
  - COLP/COFA records to demonstrate their decision-making process; and
  - evidence of regular communication with the partners.

Other risk management roles
There are some risk management roles that will be mandatory if the relevant conditions apply. For example:
- A nominated officer (also known as the money laundering reporting officer (MLRO) and in some firms a money laundering compliance officer (MLCO) as well) in circumstances where a firm is performing relevant business in the regulated sector. In the broadest of terms, this role-holder has a legal duty to report knowledge and suspicions to the National Crime Agency.

  Sitting behind this duty, there is the need to be confident that systems and processes are appropriate for managing the risks of breaching this legal duty. Does the firm have adequate risk measures in place to avoid the danger of assisting in criminal offences related to money laundering and terrorist financing activities? This is a crucial component of the firm's regulatory, compliance and ethics response and is described in more detail in Chapter 10.
- A data protection officer (DPO), in certain circumstances, to comply with data protection legislation. This is a similar type of position to the MLRO, with duties to report serious data breaches to the Information Commissioner's Office. This topic is described in Chapter 11.
- An insurance distribution officer if the firm performs insurance distribution activities and in order to comply with financial services legislation and the SRA Financial Services (Scope) Rules. This role must be filled in those firms that are not directly authorised by the Financial Conduct Authority but perform exempt regulated activities under SRA supervision and arrange insurance policies for their clients and/or otherwise give advice on insurance policies.

Other roles are not mandatory but should be considered and may be adopted to supplement and support effective governance and risk management in law firms. For example, having a designated complaints handler in the firm is not unusual and makes good managerial sense. Complaints and complainers are sounding boards providing meaningful intelligence about the compliance health of the firm, particularly in terms of client care and service delivery standards. Complaint topics might disclose any regulatory flashpoints in existence. The oversight of this by one individual will support a more consistent regulatory and compliance response and may help with the detection of repeat offences that might suggest a training or other need.

Similarly, it is not uncommon to have a senior person in a role dealing with claims against the firm caused by legal mistakes. Traditionally, this person might have been called the 'risk partner' although this may now be confusing in the era of risk management with the description having a deeper meaning than simply risk and indemnity protection. Nevertheless, having an individual with the duty to liaise with aggrieved clients and the firm's insurers makes sense, promotes consistency in response, and strengthens the detection of poor practice and other considerations that might mean the right response is or could be undermined.

Employing compliance professionals

The role of compliance professionals is a recent phenomenon in the legal services industry. We have already discussed the COLP and COFA roles that are mandatory positions.

Many firms, of all sizes and types, decide for a variety of reasons to employ additional non-mandatory compliance resources to support the mandatory roles. Variously these may be quite senior roles with titles such as Head of Risk, Compliance Manager, Head of Risk and Compliance, Head of Quality or similar. These role-holders are to all intents and purposes fulfilling the COLP and COFA functions and – crucially – ensuring that the compliance officers have the support necessary to comply with regulatory expectations.

In other organisations, the COLP and COFA may be more hands-on, but delegate some of the essential functions of the roles to other colleagues. Here we are thinking about conflicts analysts, client inception teams and similar. In many ways, this is a credible use of resources; a team of compliance professionals again will support consistency in terms of the risk management response. This may be a benefit to fee earners if they are able to rely on others to complete these important functions. However, this must be managed carefully and with the right messages conveyed to the fee earners. The functions being performed by others must not be considered as administrative obligations, the fee earner should not abdicate their responsibilities in terms of risk management, and they must under no circumstances attempt to circumvent any process performed on their behalf by such colleagues.

These positions cannot replace the COLP and COFA roles; neither should the compliance officer role-holders allow themselves to be token appointments only. However, in some firms and in some circumstances, the appointment of dedicated compliance professionals provides practical solutions.

The role of a compliance professional supporting the COLP and COFA may include the following tasks:
- providing guidance to colleagues about SRA regulation;
- overseeing the firm's internal controls to ensure that they remain effective;
- audit functions;
- compiling the records that the compliance officers are obliged to make available to the SRA;
- collating data about the firm's regulatory responses; and
- monitoring for internal and external events that have an impact on risk responses.

This is an additional resource, with budgetary implications for the employer, but many firms justify the expenditure on the basis that the cost outweighs the expense of dealing with regulatory enquiries and misconduct allegations.

However, where such a position is not deemed appropriate, there are other means of supporting the compliance officer roles and the compliance function through use of external resources. For example, many firms engage compliance consultants to assist, hire independent consultants to undertake audit work, use their accountants for training and seek best practice advice from their professional indemnity insurance providers. This approach also proves to be a useful addition to the management response. The benefits of such relationships include the following:

- seeking additional professional help only when necessary;
- receiving advice from those best placed to have a good understanding of the wider market with evidence of best practice and poor practice; and
- providing further evidence to the SRA of the firm's commitment to regulatory compliance.

In more detail: the role of effective supervision

If we can agree that law firm management, effective governance and the need to have answers to risk matters all trigger the need to have role-holders, then supervisors and effective supervision must be part of the internal framework.

We have hinted at this in preceding paragraphs, and so important is the role of supervision as a risk management tool that it warrants further consideration.

The starting point must be the regulatory expectations of this role. The SRA Standards and Regulations contains the words 'supervisor', 'supervising' and 'supervision' on countless occasions. In the SRA Code of Conduct for Solicitors, Registered European Lawyers and Registered Foreign Lawyers, the SRA states at paragraph 3.5:

Where you supervise or manage others providing legal services:

(a) you remain accountable for the work carried out through them; and

(b) you effectively supervise work being done for clients.

This is supported in the SRA Code of Conduct for Firms with the inclusion, at paragraph 4.1, of the standard that the firm must have "an effective system for supervising clients' matters".

Yet none of these words is defined in the otherwise extensive glossary.

The SRA values the importance of reporting lines and peer oversight. Anyone in any managerial line or function, or indeed any other role where they have the capacity to control or influence colleagues, should consider themselves as part of the supervisory chain and be satisfied that they are competent to fulfil the regulatory and other components of these roles. Individuals holding these types of roles may find themselves needing to account for their actions (or inaction, as the case may be) regardless of any legal qualification they may hold, and law firm partners may find that they are in the spotlight, having to defend the way in which they facilitate supervision in their workplace.

In its regulatory work, the SRA compares effective supervision and inadequate supervision. In this context, one crucial point must be understood: what is effective can only realistically be decided by law firm partners. Much will depend on the types of services offered, the qualities and abilities of the workforce, the risks that have been identified, the location of the business, the clients it serves, and the means of delivering those services. Effective supervision will flush out anything that is detrimental to the provision of suitably safe and competent legal services. Only the partners can know what effective supervision truly means in their specific environment.

What is clear, however, is that regardless of one's definition of effectiveness, having no supervisory response at all, or having supervision that only means cursory file reviews and appraisals, is likely to be inadequate. Effective supervision is so much more than grudgingly and lackadaisically undertaking file reviews and appraisals.

Countless disciplinary decisions have been made in this risk-based regulatory age that illustrate how effective supervision is closely allied with the SRA's objectives. The significance of supervision in law firm management, and the role of supervision in supporting an ethical and regulatorily compliant workplace, cannot be underestimated.

Consider, for example, the SDT decision in the matter of Ms Sovani James.[15] Ms Sovani was (on appeal to the High Court) struck off the roll of solicitors, but the decision is interesting because of the tribunal's commentary about what they perceived to be mitigating factors when looking at the respondent's conduct, as this focused on the actions of the respondent's employer. Note the following:

> *Pressures suffered by management were passed down to the fee earning team who must have felt that they were carrying the weight of the world on their junior shoulders. Creating competition amongst fee earners by the monthly publication of league tables, presumably in the misplaced hope that this would increase performance, struck particular disquiet with the tribunal. It was crass to tell junior solicitors that they had to make up hours by working weekends, long evenings, Bank Holidays, and so on and requiring them to confirm that they intended to do so that day. This was a notable example of bad, ineffective, and inappropriate management. The level of micromanagement at the Firm was obvious merely from the fact that staff were expected to sign in at the start of the day and out at the end of the day. This demonstrated lack of trust in employees.*

The law firm management team and compliance officers should take steps to ensure that the risks of poor supervision are addressed in their compliance plans, and that supervision of colleagues is adequate and effective and supportive. Such steps should be taken to demonstrate oversight of the quality and safeness of the work that is undertaken on behalf of clients of the firm, and also to ensure that ethical and regulatory compliance issues are identified and dealt with in a timely manner.

What should be achieved through effective supervision? Here are some thoughts about what the supervised employee should obtain from this workplace relationship and what the supervisor should be able to take away from the role. From the supervised person's perspective, we should be able to expect they will gain the following:

- an understanding of the firm's core regulatory, compliance and ethics values;
- motivation and support to uphold these values;
- the skills to become an ambassador for the firm and to remain with the firm;
- support through mentoring;
- informal coaching to improve standards of service delivered to clients;

- a 'safe harbour' within which personal skills can be developed;
- confidence that supports improved client relations and in turn assists in the firm's commercial growth and reputation; and
- increased but ethical productivity.

Inadequate supervision will have negative consequences for the supervised individual and ultimately will do little to support the firm's compliance culture. For example:
- The employee will feel demotivated.
- The employee will not feel valued.
- Personal growth will be more difficult.
- Problems will not be discussed in a safe environment and in a timely fashion.
- Communication will not be honest.
- The supervised individual may feel less inclined to stay employed in the business.

The supervisor's gains from this relationship should include the following:
- the intelligence needed to support the firm's regulatory and ethical security;
- information about the strengths and weaknesses of a colleague that can be used in terms of that individual's personal development and assessed against the firm's risk management requirements;
- a better understanding about whether the firm's risk management strategies work;
- insights into the psyche, strengths and vulnerabilities of another employee;
- the identification of risk hot spots such as the maverick colleague, the colleague who needs training, the colleague who is currently pressured etc; and
- personal development, particularly with regard to such soft skills as coaching and mentoring, as described in the Statement of Solicitor Competence and which support the supervisor in their own growth and maturity as a lawyer and/or a senior employee.

These reflections also trigger the need to consider the support that the supervisors themselves should be entitled to expect from the firm. Considering the usefulness of this role to the firm, it is surprising that the expectations are rarely communicated and the role-holders are often not given support to develop the non-legal soft skills required.

If supervisors are to carry out their role in the business effectively what skills are necessary? The role requires far more than simply possessing the appropriate experience of a particular subject area. It extends into skills connected with effective coaching and communication qualities. Also, supervisors need training in the compliance culture that the managers and compliance officers are instilling in the business, and they need to have clear agreement about the resources, including time, that are available to them to fulfil these particular roles.

In fact, the necessary skills are described in the Statement of Solicitor Competence, which is allied to the SRA Standards and Regulations. What does a solicitor need to demonstrate in terms of their continuing competence to practice, in circumstances where the meaning of competence is taken to be "the ability to perform the roles and tasks required by one's job to the expected standards"?[16] The competencies expected include the following:

- Competency C1 – Communicate clearly and effectively, orally and in writing.
- Competency C3 – Establish and maintain effective and professional relations with other people including
  (a) Treating others with courtesy and respect
  (b) Delegating tasks when appropriate to do so
  (c) Supervising the work of others effectively
  (d) Keeping colleagues informed of progress of work, including any risks or problems
  (e) Acknowledging and engaging with others' expertise when appropriate
  (f) Being supportive of colleagues and offering advice and assistance when required
  (g) Being clear about expectations, and

(h) Identifying, selecting and, where appropriate, managing external experts or consultants.

With these regulatory expectations in mind, what knowledge, skills and characteristics should a supervisor have? Here are some:
- subject knowledge;
- knowledge of regulation and professional ethics;
- an understanding of the firm's values – in terms of regulatory response, ethics and commercially – and how these are expressed;
- an understanding of the firm's compliance systems and the processes that must be observed;
- communication skills;
- being approachable;
- fairness;
- decisiveness – the ability to be clear about the firm's expectations;
- the ability to influence the supervised person in a positive way; and
- the ability to foster a relationship built on trust and respect.

As suggested, appropriate supervisory methods will feed into and encourage many other positive behaviours in the workplace. These include monitoring and improving client care values, addressing the competencies that are expected of solicitors when delivering a proper standard of service, feeding such values into the work of all other employees, developing appropriate training regimes, and fostering the all-important virtues of openness and accountability.

Without an effective supervision strategy, law firm managers and compliance officers will find it harder to accumulate the evidence that is needed to evaluate whether systems are working, risks managed, weaknesses identified and the firm's culture embedded.

Top tips for effective supervision

The following checklist for effective supervision is taken (and adapted slightly for the purposes of this book and our domestic audience) from the website of the Legal Practitioners' Liability Committee (LPLC) with their kind permission.[17] LPLC is a provider of professional indemnity insurance to solicitors authorised in the Australian state of Victoria. Taking into account the obvious benefits of the relationship between effective trouble-spotting and risk management controls, and the reduction in negligence claims, this checklist provides a sensible commentary on what helps. Whilst it originates overseas, the points included are top tips regardless of location.

- ✔ *Treat supervision as the real and important work it is.* There are innumerable business and personal benefits to correctly supervising employees, so give supervision the time and priority it deserves. This may mean doing less direct legal work yourself.
- ✔ *Document office systems and processes.* Having policies, processes and procedures documented gives clear direction to all staff about what is expected of them. Checklists also make it easier for staff to do what is required and for you to check that they are doing what is expected.
- ✔ *Develop position descriptions for employees.* Having clear position descriptions for all employees confirms everyone's responsibilities, duties and accountabilities with measurement criteria. The position descriptions ensure staff know what they can and cannot do.
- ✔ *Use the practice management tools you have.* Your practice management system should be able to provide you with items such as operator file lists, aged billing, work in progress (WIP) information and inactive file reports. These reports will help you oversee how your employees are managing their files. You can tell a lot about what is happening on a file if there is a lot of old WIP or unpaid bills or inactivity on files. These are often a sign a file or employee is in trouble. Bear in mind that while this financial

management information can be a good indication of how a matter is progressing, it's no substitute for actually talking to the operator at regular intervals.
- ✔ *Conduct regular file audits.* Check that processes and procedures such as sending out engagement letters and making file notes are being observed. It reinforces the firm's commitment to and expectation of quality. It also allows you to pick up things you might not have found, for example that an employee is not coping and not progressing a matter.
- ✔ *Implement a process to capture complaints.* Firms that have a well documented and advertised complaints process are often able to identify warning signs that a matter is not progressing well for any number of reasons before it becomes a bigger problem. Tell clients you welcome feedback and how to express their concerns. You should also encourage internal informal systems. Your support staff, especially your receptionist, may have a real sense of what is potentially going wrong. You can tap into that resource, especially if you have a culture where everyone understands the firm's values and expectations and works together to uphold them.
- ✔ *Adapt your approach to fit the employee.* One size does not always fit all. You will need different strategies or approaches for employees with different experience levels as well as different personalities and no matter how experienced, even senior staff need some level of supervision.
- ✔ *Monitor ingoing and outgoing mail.* Do you read all incoming hardcopy mail? Do you have a policy that only partners sign outgoing mail? These are difficult questions to answer and monitoring emails is even harder. Some firms have a policy that partners still have to approve any significant emails, some require anything of substance be a PDF letter attachment to the email and some require the partner be copied into the email. Whichever policy you adopt must be complied with and regular audits conducted.

Section 1: Governance and risk management

- ✔ *Conduct regular supervision meetings.* Be proactive about holding regular face-to-face meetings with your staff as they are a crucial supervision tool. The frequency and structure of the meetings will depend on the practice area and the seniority of the employees, as well as the workload. These meetings are not related to trust – just because you trust a person implicitly doesn't mean you don't need to have these types of meetings. They are about maintaining control of the business, complying with your professional obligations and adding value to the service provided to your clients, as well as mentoring, training and giving valuable feedback to staff.
- ✔ *Properly manage regular supervision meetings*:
    - Set regular times – weekly, fortnightly or monthly.
    - Make them a priority – don't cancel unless you absolutely have to.
    - Be prepared – use your reports and data on the fee employee work to inform the meeting.
    - Aim to address each of the matters the employee has that you are responsible for – don't just address the matters the employee wants to address.
    - Review any outstanding issues from the last meeting.
    - Provide feedback on the work done – positive or constructive.
    - Use the meetings as an assessment opportunity for development – for example assess if the employee is coping with the workload and pressure, whether new or different files should be given to them and what training may be needed.

Adding systems and processes to demonstrate compliance

The SRA Authorisation of Firms Rules contain the rules that relate to a firm's continuing authorisation. These include the need to demonstrate regulatory and legal compliance. Further detail is added to this in chapter 2 of the SRA Code of Conduct for Firms (see Table 3) which describes systems and procedural standards.

There is no additional description as to what the systems and processes should look like. This is either a blessing or a disadvantage, depending on your willingness to engage in compliance planning. Careful planning is the answer with regard to this outcome: What systems, processes and controls will ensure that the partners' requirements are met, that the Code deliverables are achieved, that intelligence is gathered and solutions monitored for appropriateness and similar?

In addition, the form of recording must be decided upon. The SRA is entitled to ask for information to satisfy itself of your regulatory health at any time and your response is determined by notification, cooperation and accountability standards in the STaRs. By way of reminder: SRA Code of Conduct for Solicitors, Registered European Lawyers and Registered Foreign Lawyers, chapter 7, Cooperation and accountability.

The following checklist identifies some of the documented systems and processes that may be appropriate to support your regulatory compliance response:
- ✔ Reporting lines
- ✔ Client care policy
- ✔ Complaints handling policy
- ✔ Conflicts policy
- ✔ Confidentiality, social media, IT, data protection policies
- ✔ Policy to manage introductions and referrals
- ✔ Outsourcing policy

With some examples of systemised processes:
- ✔ Client induction process
- ✔ Conflicts search process
- ✔ Hospitality and gift registers
- ✔ Own interests register
- ✔ Central undertakings register

Final thoughts – pinch points to addressing proper governance and risk management

No one reading this book, or anyone involved in a law firm, should be under any delusions about the SRA's requirements. It is expected that all entities that are authorised – whether a sole practitioner or a global law firm – will demonstrate an appropriate response to law firm management that includes having a proper governance model and the right attitude towards the risks associated with the business.

There are a number of obstacles to demonstrating the correct response. The following table indicates what these may be and provides some solutions:

Table 6: Compliance pinch points and strategies for dealing with them

Compliance pinch point	Strategy
Lack of collective responsibility from the partnership	Regular partner-level meetings and compliance agreements in partnership deeds etc
Underestimating and/or ignoring the seriousness of the relationship with the SRA	Learning more about the SRA and ensuring that the SRA's role is understood by all members of the firm
Having a head in sand attitude to modern regulation	Read the *Law Society Gazette*, keep up to date with SRA policy and disciplinary work and ensure that this work is publicised throughout the firm
Being unable or unwilling to tackle the firm's mavericks	Training, effective supervision, monitoring and appraisal work
Not being able to roll out appropriate systems and controls	This will often be attributable to lack of knowledge, so again, training, supervision and monitoring are antidotes
Appointing inexperienced or unsuitable role-holders in risk management positions	Training and support
Inadequate or no supervision	As above

continued on next page

Compliance pinch point	Strategy
Not accommodating modern practice, eg, remote workers, increased use of technology, careless email usage, outsourcing	Identifying the risks, reviewing systems and monitoring
Misunderstanding the importance of having demonstrable compliance procedures	Education about the role of the SRA and risks attached to lack of audit trail
Not having the confidence that all colleagues understand the internal compliance expectations	Delivering the messages with partnership-level commitment being demonstrated
The risks of assuming that your colleagues understand the regulatory position	Training
Not keeping up to date with regulatory thinking	Regular review of SRA resources and *Law Society Gazette*

In more detail: don't forget your non-solicitors

In the list above, we have suggested that working with colleagues who do not have legal training can be an obstacle to effective law firm management. Perhaps a better assessment is that it makes management more challenging or interesting! The benefits of employing a diverse group of people with a variety of different skills is ultimately a good thing – we provide services to a diverse client base and the skills that are needed in the modern law firm extend far beyond what solicitors are taught in the law school environment.

The employment mix in most law firms is a fact of life and a very common pinch point when considering the objectives that must be achieved in respect of regulation, compliance and ethics. The risk is that there will be an assumption that non-lawyers understand regulatory expectations. Nevertheless, your response to management and proper governance requirements must cover all members of the law firm and not just the solicitors.

There are two reasons for this. First, the SRA's regulatory reach extends to everyone employed within the law firm because it authorises the law firm to provide legal services. Its public interest and public protection duties mean that it has to evaluate the risk that anyone in the authorised entity presents to it or the public. It has statutory powers that enable it to expect everyone in the firm to comply with the SRA Standards and Regulations. The use of the ubiquitous "you" in the STaRs does, in the majority of sections, extend to managers and employees who are not solicitors or otherwise directly licensed by the SRA.

The consequences for the individual are that they may be the subject of enforcement action instigated by the SRA. Orders can be made prohibiting their employment in SRA-authorised law firms without SRA permission. The consequence for the solicitors and managers who employed the errant individual is scrutiny over their governance and risk management measures. Why did the non-solicitor behave in the way they did?

Secondly, there are commercial and reputational consequences if a non-solicitor working in the law firm misunderstands what is expected of them and this will have a direct consequence for the firm that employs them and expects them to act as an ambassador for all the values and standards the firm champions.

It is a risk to assume that all employees will understand what is expected of them and it is a sensible risk management response to invest time in educating your non-solicitor colleagues (who increasingly are greater in number than the solicitors within the business) so that there are assurances about their contributions to the firm's continuing authorisation. Without such training, there are no guarantees about what these individuals may do, knowingly or otherwise, that may jeopardise the firm itself.

Take, for example, the legal language in use in the business. We have in our legal language such abbreviations as SRA, TLS, LeO, COLP, COFA, NCA, SARs and more. We expect everyone to understand these but, quite honestly, why should they if they are new to our world? Explanations will remedy the different starting point.

The same is true of regulatory and ethical standards. Most employees will want to be good colleagues but will non-lawyers understand that in a law firm this includes the need to sign up to and demonstrate professional behaviours? Why should we assume that they would understand this? Why should we expect non-lawyers to appreciate the enormous burdens of the duty of confidentiality or the fact that if they promise to do something then this may be regarded as an undertaking?

Law firm managers and compliance professionals must have confidence that all colleagues are team players. Safety messages are vital, both to give confidence to the individuals and to ensure that they are effective team players and safe pairs of hands.

This is an essential exercise; it is vital when you consider that a law firm's right to open its doors every day is singularly dependent on its continuing authorisation.

Everyone must hear the same messages when they join the law firm and these messages must be communicated and understood from day one. Too often, the induction process is regarded as the responsibility of the human resources team and connected with employment matters. This misses the point that the individual is being inducted into the ways of a regulated business with professional standards and other duties that must be understood.

From day one, the regulatory, compliance and ethical communications should deliver the following key statements:

- You are working in a regulated business. That's a different experience from working in an advertising company or department store or wherever you last worked.
- The SRA is interested in everyone in the law firm and anyone could find themselves having to explain their actions to the regulator.
- Even solicitors do not have unlimited rights; these individuals only get a certificate and the right to practice for a year at a time.
- Clients must have confidence in law firms. We keep their secrets (okay, most of the time and we do need to explain the legal exceptions to this concept); we put clients' interests first; our word is our bond; and we don't allow anything or anyone to cloud our judgement. We are expected to behave professionally.
- Holding other people's money is a big deal. Clients need to be able to trust us to keep their money safe and there are complicated regulatory hoops we need to jump through.
- Things go wrong. An email will be sent to the wrong person and the knee-jerk reaction must not be to try to hide that fact.
- The firm has compliance officers with very particular roles in ensuring

that things that go wrong are recorded and that conversations are started with the SRA at the right time. It's important to know who the COLP and COFA are.
- It's equally important to know that managers and compliance officers are not telepathic so how to, and when to, tell them about things that have gone wrong, or that worry the individual, is important.

AN INSIDER'S INSIGHT

Valentina Zoghbi was until recently the Head of Risk and Compliance for CMS Cameron McKenna Nabarro Olswang LLP and a member of the Risk and Audit Committee. She was based in London and was responsible for risk management, professional risk and regulatory compliance across CMS offices in the UK, Europe, Asia and the Middle East. Valentina is a qualified lawyer and has been working within risk and compliance in the UK for over 10 years. She is an active member of the International Bar Association (IBA) and serves as a chair of the Regulation of Lawyers' Compliance Committee. In addition, she is a member of the Advisory Board of the Professional Ethics Committee and the IBA Presidential Task Force on Cyber Security.

Q: Can you provide a brief description of your firm; for example, how many staff are employed (legal and other staff), how many offices you have, what type of services are provided?

We are an international law firm with member firms throughout the world and we provide clients with specialist, business-focused legal advice from 74 offices in 68 cities and 42 countries. We are the largest law firm in Europe and have the third widest geographic coverage of any law firm in the world. Clients benefit from our leading expertise in six core sectors – Energy, Financial Services, infrastructure and project finance, lifesciences and healthcare, real estate and technology, media and telecommunications.

In May 2017, the UK member firm completed the largest-ever merger in the UK legal market with the coming together of CMS, Nabarro and Olswang. The new firm has over 450 partners in CMS Cameron McKenna Nabarro Olswang LLP (CMS) and over 2,000 lawyers in the UK with 4,500 lawyers across the world and a total staff of over 7,500.

The answers below are in relation to CMS as opposed to the wider CMS member firms.

Q: How is the firm's commitment to regulation, compliance and ethics demonstrated in practice?

CMS's commitment to regulation, compliance and ethics is demonstrated by senior management leadership, communication, training and education, reward and recognition and a well-respected risk function.

A consistent tone from the top is a key ingredient in setting our firm's values, principles and ethical culture. Senior management are accountable for oversight and management of culture and are committed to agreed risk appetite and tolerances. Culture and its impact in risk management is an ongoing board agenda item and is used to investigate new opportunities. Our risk culture is one that enables and rewards individuals for taking the right risks in an informed manner.

Face-to-face education and awareness using practical examples of situations and decisions people may face for all staff, including new joiners, and regular refresher training for trainees, NQs, partners and support departments, are critical. Staff training is mandatory, accessible, relevant and entertaining, with senior management buying into it.

Internal and external communication is key to ensuring that a consistent message about the culture and risk management of the firm is communicated to employees, clients and regulators. There is a clear focus on open communication avoiding a blame culture.

Risk management skills and knowledge are valued, encouraged and developed in the appraisal process and promotion criteria.

Section 1: Governance and risk management

Q: What does proper governance look like in your firm?
CMS has taken steps to design a governance structure that supports a risk culture. The Management Committee is the main risk management body of the firm, with the Audit & Risk Committee providing oversight of management decisions on behalf of the board. The remit of the Audit & Risk Committee is:
- to act as a focal point for the promotion of a professional and best practice culture within CMS;
- to act as a catalyst for the development among all staff of an awareness of the importance to the firm's overall business objectives of ensuring best practice so as to improve the level of commitment to delivering a high quality service to clients;
- to consider and contribute to the implementation of both firm-wide and network-wide risk management initiatives with the objective of improving the firm's and CMS network's claims record;
- to contribute to the development of sound policies and procedures on professional standards and ethical and compliance matters, so as to ensure that CMS firms have in place the necessary guidelines to enable them to comply with local regulatory requirements, standards and guidelines relevant to their business; and
- to provide practical guidance to partners and fee earners on professional standards and ethical and compliance matters, so as to ensure that the firm's policies are implemented.

In addition to the Risk and Audit Committee, the firm has a specialist Conflicts Committee. This committee is responsible for the formulation and application of the firm's policy and procedures on conflicts of interest, particularly in relation to commercial conflicts.
Team leaders (eg, practice group leaders, office managing partners, sector group leaders and business support heads) have responsibility for managing risks relating to specific matters or projects on a day to-day

"Law firm managers and compliance professionals must have confidence that all colleagues are team players. Safety messages are vital, both to give confidence to the individuals and to ensure that they are effective team players and safe pairs of hands."

basis in accordance with firm policy. They also have responsibility for promoting risk awareness within their teams.

Q: The firm has over 400 partners worldwide, so how do you ensure that there is partnership commitment to the compliance objectives?
Compliance within CMS is everyone's responsibility and is part of the firm's culture.

Internal and external communication is key to ensuring that a consistent message about the culture and risk management of the firm is communicated to employees, clients and regulators. There is a clear focus on open communication, avoiding a blame culture. Risk achievements are noted and near misses are learned from.

We ensure that there is partnership commitment to the compliance objectives by the following means:
- raising the profile of the risk team through attending departmental team meetings;
- delivering thematic awareness campaigns (eg, cyber security awareness month);
- travelling to different offices for education and training purposes;
- having a culture of approachability;
- using the services of a specialist internal marketing team to create a risk team branding with newsletters, posters, and up-to-date relevant risk intranet pages;
- having intuitive email distribution lists;
- keeping abreast of and publishing recent cases, lessons learned and near misses; and
- having risk champions in all offices.

Q: How do you ensure that partners' compliance expectations are met by all your colleagues?
Start with partners. If they walk the walk then the message is far easier

to spread. The converse is also true. Have clear supervision obligations. Send the message out through departments and in a practical way. It is more likely to stick than a message that just comes from Risk.

Q: In your view, what is necessary to have a successful compliance culture?

An effective risk culture is one that enables and rewards staff for taking the right risks in an informed manner. A successful compliance culture would include:

- *A clear commitment to ethical principles – start with ethics and start at the top.*
- *A well-respected and resourced compliance function proportionate to the size of the firm.*
- *Governance, leadership and effective board reporting. Clear leadership and tone from the top – senior management have the greatest influence in driving a particular culture. You need to inform the board regularly of upcoming regulation changes, involve them in decision making and highlight particular key risks to the business.*
- *Performance management: make everybody accountable for compliance. Everyone in the firm must be made aware that compliance is their job and responsibility.*
- *Provide incentives/compensation. Despite your best efforts, people are far more likely to take compliance seriously if they are clear as to what they stand to gain. Make sure your approaches to pay and reward reflect the behaviours you want to see. If employees know that career advancement depends on it, they know it is important.*
- *Incident reporting. Having clear processes for reporting breaches is essential.*
- *Effective communication. Get everyone on the same page and on board. Encourage everyone in the firm to communicate ideas, initiatives and ways to work better. Transparency and clear*

messages around conduct are vital. Cultivate an environment where people feel safe bringing up concerns.
- Create defined organisation structures with clear roles, responsibilities and accountability. Hold responsible those employees, even senior management, who do not meet the compliance standards of the firm.
- Proper resources and effective technology. A compliance programme is only as good as the people and technology that support it. You need effective technology and automated processes to improve compliance efficiency and effectiveness.
- Awareness. Ongoing regulatory training ensures that everyone is aware of the latest requirements.
- Auditing and monitoring. Effective compliance functions must be accountable, so structures need to be in place to ensure the right level of oversight, monitor internal systems and verify compliance. Internal or external audits provide assurances that policies and procedures are being correctly followed.
- Risk champions and global compliance committee. This assists in establishing a healthy compliance culture that permeates the entire firm and also helps you to keep abreast of local requirements.

Q: What messages would you give to anyone thinking about managing compliance in their own workplace? For example, are there any quick wins? What works and what doesn't when you are involved in managing compliance?

Start with facts. Analyse claims, complaints and 'swerves'. Do some targeted audits. 'Say what you do, do what you say, check that you have done it': most firms are good at the first part of the quality cycle, but it is also important to complete the other parts.

You should take a hard look at your training, senior management involvement and messaging with your compliance programmes and ensure your policies promote a culture of compliance.

Some of the quick wins include the following:
- *Create an explicit link between compliance, performance management and value. Consider ethics and compliance in performance role and appraisals for partners and fee earners. Special recognition (ie, leadership opportunities) should be granted to staff who demonstrate risk awareness.*
- *Consider ethics and compliance track records before promoting staff to partner or other senior leadership roles.*
- *Encourage and support a no blame culture except when wrongdoing is intentional, concealed or clearly unethical.*
- *Decline business where it is not aligned to the firm's ethical values and principles.*
- *Create a culture of compliance that fosters ethical behaviour and decision making.*
- *Empower employees to make ethical decisions and ensure people are comfortable raising concerns.*
- *Create a culture where everyone has responsibility for doing the right thing, because it is the right thing to do.*
- *Promote peer commitment – supporting each other to do the right thing this time and every time.*
- *Carry out appropriate due diligence in hiring, promotions and mergers.*
- *Manage compliance as a programme, not a project. Regulatory compliance must be ongoing.*

Q: What doesn't work?
- *Compliance for its own sake and without an ethics component.*
- *Adopting a policy and then ignoring it or applying it inconsistently. Make the policies simple, accessible and user-friendly and ensure that they are communicated to all staff.*
- *Adopting a one-size-fits-all approach to training. Training should be tailored to meet the risk profile of the specific group being trained. Make your training engaging and include follow-*

ups. Practical exercises where employees learn by doing can be very effective and fun. Don't be limited to e-learning.
- Ignoring violations by senior employees while disciplining more junior ones.
- Failing to conduct training when needed to correct any deficiencies and identify new or updated controls and procedures.
- Focusing on what people cannot do. Lists of dos and don'ts can be helpful, but start with the dos.

Q: What are the benefits of compliance to the law firm?

A robust compliance culture means queries are raised earlier and can be dealt with more quickly and effectively, which limits the damage and reduces the risks and costs involved in dealing with regulators and potential reputational damage. The benefits are many and include the following:
- Building trust with clients and creating competitive advantages and improved business opportunities. The firm's commitment to doing business the right way, to the highest ethical standards, is demonstrated.
- Greater efficiency. The more compliance is embedded in the firm the more efficient tasks become.
- Quality improvements and reduced firm and individual risk. A good compliance programme should help prevent and detect failures at an early stage, avoiding the cost that comes with regulatory investigations
- Protected reputation, which is the firm's key asset.
- An enhanced relationship with regulators and other stakeholders.
- Increased employee morale and higher retention. A well-instituted compliance programme can help in attracting and retaining talent as people want to stay in a firm that has strong values. The more employees feel they work in a fair, professional environment, the more likely they will be to stay with you.

- *Better data for informed investment, planning and expansion decisions.*
- *Higher quality information. Integrating compliance allows management to make informed decisions more rapidly.*

Q: Is there anything else you'd like to add about your experiences?

Risk, compliance and business protection are all in the same tent but need different approaches and are often done by different people. Compliance is really 'just do it' but risk management is more subtle and often on a one-to-one basis.

It is also important to consider operational risk and the importance of working with support departments, for example with the HR department over starters/transfers/leavers, the IT team over information security and data privacy impact assessments, BD over data protection/marketing risk, and procurement over third party supplier's risk.

Key points from Section 1

Managing in practice – the golden rules
- Have confidence that you know the strengths and weaknesses of your business model – evaluate the risks. What will close us down? What will cause us regulatory, reputational and/or commercial damage?
- Devise appropriate risk management strategies.
- Pitch your regulatory, compliance and ethical tone correctly and ensure that all colleagues understand what this is and what is expected of them. Tell your clients what this is – it's a selling point for the business.
- Know your partners – know that you can trust them to 'talk the talk and walk the walk' in matters relating to regulation, compliance and ethics.
- Take time to construct a governance structure that is practical and works for you.
- Ensure that there is a clear understanding about roles and responsibilities by both the role-holders and their colleagues.
- Ensure effective supervision – support your supervisors and ensure that this is a meaningful exercise with benefits for both parties and for the firm.
- Be confident that you can demonstrate accountability. Do the partners know what is happening in their name? Would you have evidence of what you do that will support your relationships with the SRA, your clients and other interested parties?
- Invest resources in delivering your regulatory, compliance and ethics messages to all colleagues – it is an investment in the longevity of your firm.
- Review and reflect – continuously. What works, what doesn't, what could we improve?

Section 2:
Demonstrating regulatory compliance in practice

Introduction

In order to stay busy, to remain entitled and authorised to provide legal services, it is necessary to know what regulatory standards must be displayed in the work that you perform and how you will demonstrate them.

In the first section of the book, we described the importance of effective management in the workplace. We have established that the SRA requires evidence that the entities it authorises (whether an individual solicitor authorised as a sole practitioner, a business owned by solicitors, or an alternative business structure with a hybrid ownership extending to non-lawyers) are well-run businesses with proper governance plans so that risks are identified, managed and mitigated.

This is the foundation on which the next stage of an effective and appropriate regulatory relationship will be built. The next building block is the ability to prove to the SRA that this well-run business is an arena in which compliance with regulatory requirements is enabled.

This section is devoted to regulatory compliance in practice, a phrase overused and very familiar but not always analysed by the user. What does it actually mean? What does the SRA want to see from authorised people who must respond to this expectation, and what should we witness in well-run law firms?

In the broadest of introductory overviews, regulatory compliance is the response to the various principles, rules and other requirements that the SRA shares with us in its regulatory toolkit, the SRA Standards and Regulations. An individual solicitor must abide by these requirements in order to remain certified and able to practise law. Law firm managers must create the right environment in their businesses in which these requirements can be met and in order that there are no regulatory challenges to the business's authorised status and ability to provide legal services.

In more detail, it is clear that this is sometimes a complex and intricate requirement that demands more on the part of the individual solicitor and law firm manager than simply reading the SRA STaRs. It requires an understanding of ethics and what constitutes ethical behaviour.

There are at least two challenges that make this requirement difficult to achieve:

- The regulatory requirements are designed to ensure that we meet appropriate standards and deliver safe services to our clients, and that the public perception of the profession as a trustworthy one remains untarnished. This requires an understanding that significant sections of the SRA STaRs originate in ethical behaviours; individual managers and employees must act ethically and law firms must create a working environment in which ethical behaviour is acceptable and normal. It is harder for an individual to act ethically where ethics is not part of the firm's psyche and it is harder for a law firm to provide the necessary assurances to the SRA that it is a safe entity when it houses individuals who do not act ethically.

- The regulator is required to test us against the standards that have been set. Failure to achieve these standards may mean that enforcement and disciplinary action will be initiated against us. This requires both an understanding of the basic behavioural duties and an awareness of how these are applied by the SRA and, at times, the courts.

In practical terms, this means that we need to be able to demonstrate how we achieve the requirements and to identify when things go wrong. The SRA Code of Conduct for Firms includes a mandatory requirement that authorised bodies (ie, your SRA-authorised law firm) must have suitable arrangements for compliance,[18] records of compliance and the ability to report serious breaches promptly to the SRA.[19] These duties explain why it is necessary for modern law firms to implement effective systems, controls and processes.

One of the motivating forces for regulatory emphasis in our behaviours is the fact that we are required to act as trusted advisers. We are expected to be trustworthy. If we do not have the correct regulatory, compliance and ethical infrastructure in place, our reputation as trusted individuals, and collectively an honourable profession, may be harder to prove.

The message is clear: we have the role of trusted advisers and this is the non-negotiable basis upon which all regulatory, client and other relationships are based. Nothing and no one should be allowed to compromise the correct regulatory and ethical starting point. This is what sustains our reputation.

Case study

Consider the case of an individual solicitor who failed to demonstrate that he had met the requirements of the SRA and, as a consequence, was fined £305,000 by the SDT, ordered to pay costs of £37,016.10 and struck off the roll of solicitors. At the time of writing, this is the largest fine imposed by the SDT against an individual.

The solicitor was Mr Nigel Harvie. The SRA reported the case as follows:[20]

- *[Mr Harvie] entered into a financial arrangement with a former client without advising her to take independent advice, and*

"*The message is clear: we have the role of trusted advisers and this is the non-negotiable basis upon which all regulatory, client and other relationships are based.*"

where his own interests conflicted or potentially conflicted with the interests of the former client.
- He acted towards his former client in a way that was contrary to his position as solicitor.

Mr Harvie denied that he used his position as a solicitor to take unfair advantage for himself or another party, but the SDT upheld this allegation as well.

In return for paying for the care and living costs of a lady, for whom he had acted previously, Mr Harvie acquired ownership of her house. The house was valued at £300,000 in 2005 when the arrangement began and over the next five years, Mr Harvie paid out in the region of £200,000.

The house was never valued again and the arrangement came to an end in 2010 when the former client died. The Land Registry recorded the value of the house at £800,000 in 2012.

The client had declared in her will that her estate should be used to set up a trust fund to help foreign students, but this has not happened. The matter was only discovered when neighbours of the deceased complained to the SRA that her wishes had not been carried out.

Mr Harvie asserted that the deceased lady had only been his client when he prepared her will for her in 2004, and that she was happy with the arrangement. He also claimed the co-executor of her estate was aware of his actions at all times.

In delivering the sanction, the tribunal said they were taking a very serious view of the circumstances of this matter. It also said the public would be appalled by the behaviour of Mr Harvie in taking unfair advantage of his former client and he had done significant harm to the reputation of the profession.

David Middleton, Executive Director for Legal and Enforcement, said: "The SRA is committed to working with solicitors and firms to raise standards and uphold core professional principles. Solicitors occupy unique positions of trust often on behalf of vulnerable members of the public.

> "Mr Harvie abused that trust, and the record level of the fine clearly reflects the seriousness of this betrayal. Although Mr Harvie stated that his former client was happy with the arrangement put in place, he should have ensured that she seek independent advice at the outset because he stood to gain financially and therefore there was a clear conflict of interest."

In this section, we will take this regulatory expectation as our starting point and describe the essential knowledge that must be applied and demonstrated in the practice of law. This means that individuals must know what behaviours they must demonstrate and the firm must encourage and monitor these behaviours

It may be stating the obvious, but these behaviours must be applied to all aspects of the client retainer. Regulation is designed on a model that is consumer-focused so that our compliance methodologies must demonstrate to the regulator how we focus on these objectives when providing legal services.

This concept requires an understanding of the basic ethical knowledge and the standards that must be met in all solicitor/law firm relationships with the client. 'Client care' is the generic term for what we are describing. In practice, this phrase is often interpreted narrowly and only applied to the specific requirements that arise from the contractual arrangements with a client and used to explain standards of service. When used more comprehensively, the term incorporates ancillary considerations such as whether we can act in a client's best interests. Do we have a conflict of interest? Can we make full disclosure of all material matters? Can we keep client matters private (confidentiality) and deliver services of an acceptable standard (competency considerations, suitable undertakings etc)? For this reason, basic ethical knowledge is described in this section, with suggestions about how to achieve the best environment in which to ensure that the correct behaviour is not compromised.

We will also consider the challenges to achieving these behaviours and satisfying the regulator that we are providing safe services. These challenges may be internal distractors such as financial motivators or lack of awareness or diligence on the part of colleagues, and/or may derive from external pressures such as those arising in respect of client expectations about what we will do for them and the instructions that they can give us.

A particularly visible risk pinch point when it comes to demonstrating regulatory compliance in practice arises in respect of litigation and the use of the court. This work stream is a regulatory and ethical hot spot for various reasons. Litigation and advocacy are reserved activities and we (along with other qualified persons) are trusted to use court facilities where others do not have such an entitlement; litigation is an area of law where our clients must have confidence that we are acting in their best interests; and the court is an additional stakeholder, evaluating our behaviours and highlighting concerns to our regulator. Adopting the wrong response has regulatory and reputational repercussions. The tensions will be highlighted, with strategies for the correct response.

Such challenges must not be allowed to gain momentum. In fact, the value of receiving services from law firms that conform to regulatory standards, and that are rooted in ethical behaviours, ought to be a positive attribute that is promoted to clients and used to enhance a firm's reputation. Being able to demonstrate the correct regulatory, compliance and ethical perspective is good for business. This concept is also discussed in this section and tested against the regulatory and ethical decisions that must be made throughout a retainer. This last point dispels the myth, common in many firms, that regulatory compliance considerations can be dealt with as an administrative function tied up with client acceptance processes. This is not true.

Finally, we conclude this section with top tips and a plan to ensure that regulatory compliance values are demonstrated in practice.

Chapter 2:
What is ethics?

Introduction

If we accept that regulatory compliance has many of its origins in ethical behaviours, and that there is a need to satisfy the SRA that you and your firm represent a safe, ethical environment that it can safely authorise and from which clients can receive legal services, then the starting point must be an agreement about what we mean by the concept of 'ethics'.

AN INSIDER'S INSIGHT

Francisco Esparraga is a senior lecturer at the School of Law, University of Notre Dame in Sydney, Australia. His reflections on this topic are a perfect scene-setter for our further deliberation about what matters and what we must facilitate within our law firms.

Ethical behaviour – a few thoughts
Most people are ethical. Most lawyers are ethical. Whilst we all make poor decisions from time to time, that does not make us unethical. Yet, many people are much more cynical when it comes to ethical behaviour in our society, particularly in business and in the law.

The commitment made by lawyers on admission to the legal

profession is not simply to abide by a set of rules, but to commit to honesty and integrity and as such, ethical behaviour matters. To quote Abraham Lincoln, a lawyer before becoming president of the USA: "You must remember that some things legally right are not morally right."

Legal ethics is about the intersection of ethics and the actual practice of legal professionals. It is about analysing what can and should be done and what is right and what is wrong. It is about promoting certain modes of moral reasoning and conduct. It is concerned with both the practice and the theory. One cannot exist without the other. As such, it matters.

Legal ethics is the application of general moral principles to the practice of law. It is a combination of Ethics – the set of rules that describes what is acceptable; Values – the acts, customs and institutions regarded in a favourable way; Morals – the set of rules or mode of conduct considered universal; Integrity – honesty and sincerity and the ability to be trusted; Character – driving what we do when no one is looking; and Laws – the rules and regulations setting the boundaries of behaviour. It is generally accepted that what is law and what is morally right should coincide, hence the importance of ethical behaviour.

It is for this reason that almost universally, professional rules targeted at lawyers intertwine ethical behaviour and as such, lawyers must:

- *act honestly and fairly in a client's best interest;*
- *not engage in or assist in conduct that is calculated to defeat the ends of justice or otherwise in breach of the law;*
- *act with due skill and diligence;*
- *act with reasonable promptness;*
- *maintain client confidences;*
- *avoid conflicts of interest;*
- *refrain from charging excessive legal costs;*
- *act with honesty and candour in all dealings with courts and tribunals;*
- *observe any undertakings given; and*

- act with honesty, fairness and courtesy in all affairs including dealings with other practitioners, law firms and the community.

Clearly, in all aspects of the lawyer's professional work, there is a need for ethical behaviour.

Ethical behaviour is important for success in business, the law and society in general. It is not just a question of personal integrity but also a question of ethical management within organisations such as law firms. Law firms should be values-based by using both formal and informal accountability to create an ethical culture. Enforceable codes of ethics should be integrated within law firms with top management commitment.

The top management in law firms has the opportunity to demonstrate moral leadership through personal behaviour and through the environment it creates for staff. To operate an ethical organisation such as a law firm, you have to create an environment that allows staff to operate in an ethical manner.

Top management must set the tone by what it does, how it does it and how it sets the boundaries for acceptable behaviour. In short, the values professed by top management must be aligned with demonstrated behaviour. There must be zero tolerance for unethical behaviour. There is no point having codes of ethics within an organisation without a demonstration of real consequence. Ethical conduct needs to be rewarded and continually reinforced.

Chapter 3:
Essential behaviour

Introduction

One word sums up the sentiments in the introduction to this section: trust. The client (and more generally, the public) assumes that they will be able to trust solicitors and everyone working with solicitors in law firms.

Having trust in someone – or something – is of course subjective. Do we have faith in someone, can we count on them, will they do the right thing? The belief that solicitors, and law firms, can be relied upon to always do the right thing is at the core of the public's expectations of the profession and at the heart of regulation, compliance and ethics.

The practicalities are that whilst this starting point is subjective, the regulatory role is such that the question of trust must be converted into something that is standardised and can be tested against stated objectives. The SRA has duties to oversee our response to the requirement to act as trusted advisers and to ensure that the response from all solicitors and all law firms is consistent. For this reason, the SRA's regulatory toolkit contains a number of mandatory requirements designed to ensure that we fulfil the expectations imposed upon us.

Grasping the fundamental expectations

The SRA is authorised to ensure that the regulatory objectives in the

Legal Services Act 2007 are put into practice. Trust is at the core of these objectives, which include such requirements as the duty to protect and promote the interests of consumers and to promote and maintain adherence to professional principles.

A reminder of the professional principles[21] directed at authorised persons in terms of the Legal Services Act 2007:
- You should act with independence and integrity.
- You should maintain proper standards of work.
- You should act in the best interests of your clients.
- If you exercise rights of audience before any court, or conduct litigation in relation to proceedings in any court, by virtue of being an authorised person, you should comply with your duty to the court to act with independence in the interests of justice.
- You must keep the affairs of clients confidential.

The professional principles and the SRA's regulatory toolkit

The Legal Services Act 2007 is one of the SRA's main source materials for its regulatory toolkit. It takes the legal requirements, including the professional principles, and uses these to ensure that its work supports its regulatory objectives and its mandate to create safe service standards against which we are tested.

In order to avoid challenge, we must understand the behaviours that the SRA expect us to demonstrate.

The SRA Principles 2019

First and foremost, we are all expected to comply with the SRA Principles. This is a collection of mandatory values that the SRA endorses in the following way:

The SRA Principles comprise the fundamental tenets of ethical behaviour that we expect all those that we regulate to uphold. This includes all individuals we authorise to provide legal services (solicitors, RELs and RFLs), as well as authorised firms and their managers and employees. For licensed bodies, these apply to those individuals, and the part of the body (where applicable), involved in delivering the services we regulate in accordance with the terms of your licence.[22]

Such is the importance of the Principles to an individual's, or the firm's, relationship with the SRA that they are referenced throughout the narrative of this book. It is important to understand them all and apply them as necessary in practice:

You act:
1. *in a way that upholds the constitutional principle of the rule of law, and the proper administration of justice;*
2. *in a way that upholds and confidence in the solicitors' profession and in legal services provided by authorised persons;*
3. *with independence;*
4. *with honesty;*
5. *with integrity;*
6. *in a way that encourages equality, diversity and inclusion; and*
7. *in the best interests of each client.*

Whilst the "you" described in each Principle requires an individual response from every individual (qualified or otherwise) in the business, proper governance and risk management expectations should generate an internal conversation about the firm's required collective response between all the individuals who make up the business. The collective response must be monitored to ensure that there is understanding, acceptance, and consistency. It is important to understand that in some circumstances, the Principles also extend to our personal lives and allow the SRA to consider actions in this context.

The table below sets out management questions that must be debated in order to ensure that there is the basis on which to develop the safety net of such a collective response.

Section 2: Demonstrating regulatory compliance in practice

Table 7: The Principles – questions and debate

Principle	Managerial questions
Principle 1: Upholding the rule of law	This duty requires an unequivocal response. Individual duties to use the court function properly must not be undermined. In our private lives, our duty to uphold the rule of law must be understood and the SRA must be made aware of certain reportable matters. Your questions: How do we ensure that we manage client expectations about the limits of what we can legally and ethically do for them? Have we created the right environment in which our colleagues are empowered to challenge inappropriate behaviour that may compromise this duty? Have we educated our colleagues so that they understand personal reporting duties?
Principle 2: Trust in the profession	This behaviour is often considered in disciplinary matters – has an individual behaved in such a way (either professionally or in their private life) that trust in them or the profession as a whole is placed in jeopardy? Your questions: Have we made our expectations about what will be considered untrustworthy behaviour clear? Are we monitoring our colleagues to ensure that we can be confident that they will behave properly? Do we communicate these expectations clearly and often and does this extend to reminders about the expectation that they will behave impeccably at all times including at social events and through all mediums such as when using social media? Have we made it clear that we expect openness and accountability, and that all colleagues must be aware of the need to identify inappropriate behaviour in themselves and in others?
Principle 3: Independence	This Principle has many nuances that must be acknowledged. It applies individually and to the firm as a business. Your questions: Have we identified who, or what, could make it difficult to demonstrate our ability to act without compromise? Have we stated our expectations that this duty will not be compromised so that we empower our colleagues to challenge such potentially harmful relationships or situations? Do we have measures in place to ensure that these risks are monitored and managed?

continued on next page

Principle	Managerial questions
Principle 4: Honesty	This duty was included in the Principles in November 2019 under the SRA Standards and Regulations. The SRA does not give us a regulatory definition of this but says in guidance: "The courts have made clear that the standard of honesty required for solicitors is that they may be 'trusted to the ends of the earth' (*Bolton v Law Society* [1993] EWCA Civ 32)."[23] Your questions: Do we make sufficient enquiry of new employees? Have we made it clear that we expect to be notified about all issues connected with dishonesty that might arise in an employee's professional or private life? Do we supervise colleagues to ensure honesty in their actions? Do we have sufficient controls of client money and client accounts?
Principle 5: Integrity	Integrity is used as a benchmark by the SRA and other stakeholders to verify confidence in the trustworthiness of individuals and the profession. However, its regulatory meaning has largely developed through SDT disciplinary work and case law. The risks attached to this vagueness are increased in an environment where the managers of the law firm have not clearly expressed their expectations about the behaviours which they expect from colleagues. When considering the difference between honesty (Principle 4) and integrity, the SRA says: "Whilst someone acting dishonestly can be said to be acting without integrity, the concept of integrity is wider than just acting dishonestly. This means that it is possible to behave without integrity without necessarily being dishonest."[24] Your questions: Have we an agreed statement about the qualities we expect to see in all colleagues in practice? Have we helped colleagues with their understanding of how their actions will uphold the values in this statement? Have we made it clear about the consequences of failing to meet the standards of this published statement? Do we support colleagues who identify inappropriate behaviour?

continued on next page

Section 2: Demonstrating regulatory compliance in practice

Principle	Managerial questions
Principle 6: Equality, diversity and inclusion	There are both legal and ethical duties that arise in respect of this behaviour. The SRA has published Guidance in which it says: "While legislation sets minimum legal obligations – that your firm takes steps to remove potential discrimination, harassment and victimisation – your regulatory obligations extend beyond strict compliance with the law. An inclusive approach adds value to an organisation and is increasingly recognised as a commercial imperative for business."[25] **Your questions:** Have we analysed how this Principle manifests itself in practice, in all areas of the business and in respect of all employees/prospective employees, current/former/prospective clients, and in our dealings with third parties? Have we made it clear about the behaviours that will not be tolerated either in the workplace or in any context that might have repercussions for the firm and its management? Does everyone know their specific role in supporting this Principle? Do we have appropriate policies that support this duty? Do we have suitable complaints mechanisms to deal with concerns from both colleagues and clients? Do we consider the relationships we have with third parties and how these might undermine our duties? Should we deliver training on the law, the SRA's requirements, and our internal expectations?
Principle 7: Acting in the client's best interests	Clients must have confidence that if we – individually and as a firm – agree to act on their behalf, it will be after due consideration of whether anything prevents us from providing an unfettered legal service. **Your questions:** Do we have the correct client inception processes to ensure that we can demonstrate that we have considered whether it is appropriate to act for a particular client in a specific matter? Are we confident that our means of recording own interest conflicts is meaningful? Is our method of assessing client conflict appropriate? Can we in fact demonstrate that we undertake meaningful conflict checks before we accept instructions and that all decisions to act are monitored throughout the client relationship? Are we confident that individuals take personal responsibility and accountability for conflict decisions? Have we taken firm-wide decisions about high-risk scenarios and is our position communicated to colleagues and monitored?

continued on next page

Principle	Managerial questions
	Do all colleagues understand the duty of confidentiality and do fee earners add a correct interpretation of their duty of disclosure? Have we made our position clear about the use of information barriers? Do our people understand both the regulatory requirements and our internal systems? Do we need to demonstrate this through training and monitoring? Have we added to this ethical starting point with any commercially derived decisions about our client relationships? Do these decisions feed into our client identification process? Are these decisions disseminated to the right people in the firm? Are we confident that any decisions made on a commercial basis do not create ethical dilemmas?

Applying regulatory thinking to the Principles – obstacles and misunderstandings

Managers are expected to ensure that the Principles are understood and demonstrated in the workplace. They may be asked to prove that they are factored into compliance strategies. It is a worthwhile exercise to anticipate any regulatory compliance scrutiny, demonstrating that internal systems can be mapped back to the originating Principles. The table above provides you with useful questions to inform management planning meetings.

However, do not underestimate the amount of care that must be taken and the many pitfalls to achieving this position. Putting principles into practice is not without obstacles. An effective management response will acknowledge this and provide solutions to mitigate the ensuing risks.

Two of the more common misunderstandings are as follows:
- Employees who are not directly involved in delivering services to clients may fail to appreciate the significance of these Principles both for them personally and for the role that they have in supporting the firm's continuing authorised status.

  To be clear, the Principles apply to everyone and the SRA will expect there to be effective management of this message and application in practice.

Consider the following non-solicitor roles and the values that are most directly relevant to the role-holders:

- Front of house/reception staff: acting in a client's best interests, trust and protecting client money.
- Fee earner support staff: integrity, independence, acting in a client's best interests, proper standards of service, trust, equality and diversity and protecting client money.
- The human resources team: integrity, equality and diversity.
- The learning and development/in-house trainers: integrity, equality and diversity.
- The marketing team: integrity, acting in a client's best interests, trust, equality and diversity.
- The information technology team: integrity, trust, acting in a client's best interests and protecting client money and assets.
- The accounts team: integrity, independence, trust and, of course, protecting client money.
- The director of finance/chief financial officer: all of the above, plus financial risk management.
- The practice/office manager: again, all of the above plus the need to be confident that the firm is properly governed.

This presents management with challenges. How do we ensure we have everyone on side and acting consistently? What language do we use to communicate these messages when we are dealing with non-solicitors? What training should we deliver to them? Do we actually remember to include these colleagues in our compliance responses?

A firm that can demonstrate that the significance of working in an SRA-authorised firm is made clear to prospective employees and during the induction process; that trains support staff in an appropriate manner; considers them in terms of the suitability of internal systems and controls; and monitors these colleagues' aptitude and willingness to conform, is more likely to satisfy the SRA that it is meeting regulatory expectations.

- Conflicts can arise between one or more of the duties through a misunderstanding of the weighting between the various Principles.

A useful training exercise is to ask colleagues which of the Principles they would prioritise or nominate as the most important one. The answers will provide the trainer with a useful insight into the mindset of the responder. Invariably, the answer to this question will be that Principle 7 and the duty to act in the client's best interest must be the priority action. This is not always true; it is a misunderstanding that must be debunked if the individual and the firm are to avoid the risk of regulatory scrutiny in certain circumstances.

Consider the scenario whereby it is in the client's best interests in litigation that the court, or the other side, is allowed to believe a certain argument that the fee earner actually knows is inaccurate or misleading. Would it be allowable to argue that in these circumstances, the court can be allowed to be misled because that is in the client's best interests? Of course not, but this erroneous supposition is common.

Such is the importance of this point that the SRA includes reference to it in the Principles, as follows:

Should the Principles come into conflict, those which safeguard the wider public interest (such as the rule of law, and public confidence in a trustworthy solicitors' profession and a safe and effective market for regulated legal services) take precedence over an individual client's interests. You should, where relevant, inform your client of the circumstances in which your duty to the Court and other professional obligations will outweigh your duty to them.[26]

Section 2: Demonstrating regulatory compliance in practice

Case study

The consequences of wrong weighting as between the Principles have been considered in court proceedings and have also formed the basis of regulatory disciplinary action. Consider the SDT case arising in respect of the conduct of a solicitor, Mr Alastair Brett. The case was reported by the SRA on its website in 2013 as follows:[27]

> *The Times newspaper's former legal director, Alastair Brett, will be suspended from practising for six months from 16 December by the Solicitors Disciplinary Tribunal following a prosecution by the Solicitors Regulation Authority (SRA).*
>
> *The tribunal decided to suspend Mr Brett yesterday (Thursday 5 December) after it found that he had failed to act with integrity contrary to Rule 1.02 of the Solicitors Code of Conduct 2007, and knowingly allowed the Court to be misled in the conduct of litigation contrary to Rule 11.01 of the Solicitors Code of Conduct 2007. He was also ordered to pay £30,000 costs.*
>
> *The SRA told the tribunal that in June 2009, while conducting litigation in the High Court on behalf of Times Newspapers Limited, Mr Brett knowingly or recklessly allowed a witness statement to be served in support of its defence which created a misleading impression. The Authority also said that during a hearing in that litigation before Mr Justice Eady, Mr Brett knowingly allowed the court to proceed on the basis of an incorrect assumption as to the facts.*
>
> *The litigation centred on the naming of the author of the "Nightjack" blog as serving police officer DC Horton. Patrick Foster, a journalist working for The Times, discovered Nightjack's identity by unlawful access to email accounts. Mr Brett denied the allegations, claiming he instructed Mr Foster to undertake research to demonstrate that DC Horton's identity could be ascertained through open source material, and also denied knowing when Mr Foster first began to undertake that research.*
>
> *In sanctioning Mr Brett, the tribunal described him as "a deeply unconvincing witness" who "blamed everyone but himself". It found Mr*

Brett "adopted a win at all costs approach to the Nightjack litigation".

Antony Townsend, SRA Chief Executive, said: "Solicitors hold positions of great trust, so it is essential that they act with integrity and do not allow courts to be misled. The public needs to know that if solicitors fail to uphold these standards they will be held to account."

As a postscript, it should be noted that Mr Brett appealed this decision.[28] The appeal was heard in the Divisional Court of the Queen's Bench Division. Mr Justice Wilkie ruled as follows:

I would allow this appeal by Mr Brett, but only to the extent of quashing the decision of the SDT that he was guilty of a breach of Rule 11.01 by 'knowingly' misleading the court, and substituting for it a finding that he was guilty of Rule 11.01 by 'recklessly' misleading the court.

This is a crucial point. In a recently published paper, Dr Stephen Vaughan and Emma Oakley of the University of Birmingham Law School reported the findings of their research into the ethics displayed by corporate finance lawyers.[29] Their commentary includes a highly relevant, but often overlooked, fact which refers to the SRA Handbook but is equally relevant to the SRA Standards and Regulations:

Nowhere, at no point, does the SRA say in its Handbook (or, indeed, anywhere else) that the client's interests come first.

Questions to test your colleagues' principles

It is important to be able to have confidence in your colleagues' ethical response; the firm's authorisation and reputation depend on this. It is risky not to know what response you can expect until an individual is put to an ethical test. The answer may not be to your liking!

The benefits of pre-testing your colleagues' principles may need to be explained to managers in the business who may be more interested in the business of lawyering rather than the testing of the regulatory blanket that is wrapped around their delivery of legal services.

It is easier to put compliance solutions into action when working with like-minded colleagues. A firm that is composed of a number of individuals who can be trusted to respond to regulatory and ethical matters consistently is undoubtedly a safer one in which to work. But, how will we know that we can rely on all colleagues to do the right thing and have the right responses unless these matters are discussed?

It is never too early to test an individual's regulatory and ethical viewpoint. Questions can be asked in interviews and during induction periods to ascertain the risk baggage that the individual may be bringing into the firm with them. For example, lateral hires of experienced individuals may be good commercial decisions but at the same time may also mean that the firm's regulatory solutions are in some way undermined and made less secure by any different regulatory thinking they bring with them. This must not be allowed to happen. Knowledge of an individual's default position enables the firm to make an informed decision about the overall risk of the appointment.

More generally, consider the use of the following questions to flush out more information about the prospective or newly introduced colleague:

- How do you view the regulatory relationship with the SRA?
- Why would you consider yourself to be ethical?
- How do you describe integrity?
- What do you expect in terms of the management of a law firm?
- Why do you think that trust in the profession is so important?
- What would you do if you felt uncomfortable in acting on client instructions?
- What do you understand about the duty of self-reporting serious issues about your conduct?
- What does delivering a proper standard of work mean to you?

Putting the Principles into practice – compliance with the SRA Codes of Conduct 2019

The SRA Principles are the regulatory starting point for interaction with the regulated community. This means that they are our starting point for demonstrating compliance. However, the SRA Standards and Regulations contain more than just this set of high-level duties. In respect of our behaviours in the workplace, the STaRs contain two Codes of Conduct which describe the regulator's expectations about how we will behave in practice or, to put this another way, how we deliver trustworthy and ethically based services. These Codes contain standards of professionalism that create benchmarks about how to deal with ethical decision-making which must be achieved where relevant and against which we will be tested if there are any concerns about our behaviour.

The SRA Code of Conduct for Solicitors, Registered European Lawyers and Registered Foreign Lawyers apply to these individuals who are directly and individually regulated by the SRA. In the introduction to this Code, the SRA writes:

The Code of Conduct describes the standards of professionalism that we, the SRA, and the public expect of individuals (solicitors, registered European lawyers and registered foreign lawyers) authorised by us to provide legal services.

[...]

You are personally accountable for compliance with this Code – and our other regulatory requirements that apply to you – and must always be prepared to justify your decisions and actions. A serious failure to meet our standards or a serious breach of our regulatory requirements may result in our taking regulatory action against you. A failure or breach may be serious either in isolation or because it comprises a persistent or concerning pattern of behaviour.

The second Code applies to authorised and licensed law firms and is called the SRA Code of Conduct for Firms. Again, the introductory paragraphs contain the SRA's expectations:

This Code of Conduct describes the standards and business controls that we, the SRA, and the public expect of firms (including sole practices) authorised by us to provide legal services. These aim to create and maintain the right culture and environment for the delivery of competent and ethical legal services to clients.

[...]

A serious failure to meet our standards or a serious breach of our regulatory requirements may lead to our taking regulatory action against the firm itself as an entity, or its managers or compliance officers, who each have responsibilities for ensuring that the standards and requirements are met. We may also take action against employees working within the firm for any breaches for which they are responsible. A failure or breach may be serious either in isolation or because it comprises a persistent or concerning pattern of behaviour.

A solicitor employed by or owning an authorised law firm will need to comply with both Codes, although much of the Firm Code mirrors the wording of the Individual Code. In addition, the Firm Code contains standards of professionalism which will apply to the owners of the business, it contains duties for the firm's compliance officers, and it applies to everyone else employed in the business regardless of their role.

Having a satisfactory relationship with the SRA requires us to demonstrate that we understand the Codes, what their contents are designed to achieve, and how we will demonstrate compliance in practice.

The current versions of the Codes, and the relevant standards which must be achieved, are shown in Tables 8 and 9 below:

Table 8: The SRA Code of Conduct for Solicitors, Registered European Lawyers and Registered Foreign Lawyers

Chapter	Content
1: Maintaining trust and acting fairly	Standards relating to unfair discrimination; not taking unfair advantage; undertakings; not misleading clients or the court or others
2: Dispute resolution and proceedings before courts, tribunals and inquiries	Standards that apply to your duties as an officer of the court or in other circumstances
3: Service and competence	Standards relating to client instructions; competency standards; client vulnerability and/or attributes; supervision and management

continued on next page

Chapter	Content
4: Client money and assets	Standards designed to ensure client money and assets are safeguarded
5: Referrals, introductions and separate businesses	Standards describing duties in respect of referral and introduction arrangements; duties when involved in a non-SRA-authorised business
6: Conflict, confidentiality and disclosure	Standards relating to conflicts of interests (own interests and clients' conflict); confidentiality duties; duty of disclosure; duty that arises when there is a conflict between confidentiality and disclosure
7: Cooperation and accountability	Standards relating to knowledge about law and regulation; justification of regulatory decision-making; cooperation with SRA and other stakeholders; SRA reporting duties; reporting duties to other stakeholders; duties to clients to be honest and open
8: When you are providing services to the public or a section of the public	Client care standards relating to client identification; complaints handling; client information and publicity

Table 9: The SRA Code of Conduct for Firms

Chapter	Content
1: Maintaining trust and acting fairly	Same as Individual Code plus standards relating to the monitoring, reporting and publishing of workforce diversity data
2: Compliance and business systems	Standards designed to ensure that the authorised business has effective governance structures and internal systems and controls in the workplace; record-keeping duties; monitoring financial and business viability; management of risk
3: Cooperation and accountability	Same as Individual Code plus standards that apply to notification of firm-specific information
4: Service and competence	Duties about acting on client instructions and competence, plus firm-wide standards relating to the facilitation of competence standards by all colleagues and the duty to have an effective system for supervising clients' matters

continued on next page

Section 2: Demonstrating regulatory compliance in practice

Chapter	Content
5: Client money and assets	Standards relating to the safeguarding of client money and assets
6: Conflict, confidentiality and disclosure	Same or near identical standards as in the Individual Code
7: Applicable standards in the SRA Code of Conduct for Solicitors, RELs and RFLs	Describes the other standards from the Individual Code that apply to the firm – dispute resolution and proceedings before courts etc; referrals, introductions and separate businesses; standards which apply when providing services to the public or a section of the public
8: Managers in SRA-authorised firms	NB – managers in the context means the owners of the firm and they must be aware of a standard of professionalism that states that they are responsible for compliance with this Code, and that this responsibility is joint and several if management responsibility is shared with other managers of the firm
9: Compliance officers	Standards that apply to the firm's compliance officers for legal practice, and finance and administration

Such is the importance of the content of the Codes that it is impossible to guarantee the correct response to regulatory compliance requirements without reading this section of the STaRs. However, the table below explains the key content and provides useful questions to consider as a starting point for management discussions about how to demonstrate compliance in practice.

Table 10: Questions to ask in relation to Code outcomes

Code content	Managerial questions
Client care, service and competence	This set of outcomes primarily supports your compliance with Principles 2, 5 and 7 and the duty to act as trusted advisers and in the client's best interests. Chapters 3 and 8 of the Individual Code and chapters 3 and 7 of the Firm Code describe the standards of professionalism that must be achieved in terms of delivering legal services. **Questions for you:** What type of service do we intend to offer our clients? Have we in fact identified the correct client and, if we are not communicating directly with the client, have we taken steps to ensure that third party instructions are properly authorised? Can we demonstrate that the client understands the services we will deliver and how this will be put into effect? How do we ensure that costs information is explained clearly? Do we have an appropriate complaints handling process and is the nature of complaints understood by all staff? Do we consider whether we are competent to act before taking instructions; do we include decisions about whether we can act, or continue to act, on legal and ethical grounds?
Equality, diversity and inclusion	Code standards (in chapter 1 of each Code) support Principle 6 and also address our legal duties as contained in the Equality Act 2010. Standards must be achieved by all individuals within the firm in respect of their dealings with colleagues, clients and all third parties. They also apply by implication to the individuals within the firm with responsibilities in making decisions about client services and in respect of employment matters. **Questions for you:** Do we have the confidence that we can trust our colleagues to treat each other with respect and know that these values extend to their relationships with our clients and third parties more generally? Do we make our expectations clear about the values we will not tolerate in the wider context (eg, use of social media to post offensive messages)? Do we have the means to tackle issues in the workplace and client complaints? Do we monitor third-party suppliers to ensure we are not tainted by any lesser standards that they display?

continued on next page

Section 2: Demonstrating regulatory compliance in practice

Code content	Managerial questions
Conflicts of interest	It is vital that the standards in chapter 6 of both Codes are understood properly and applied in practice. Acting against the interests of a client (whether this is because of your own interests or the interests of another client) means that Principle 7 will not have been achieved. Significantly, we are given regulatory definitions that are to be applied to both types of conflict and an outcome that makes it mandatory to have effective systems and controls to identify and assess potential conflicts of interest. Questions for you: Are we confident that the right people within the firm understand regulatory requirements, any commercial decisions which may have added to the SRA starting point, our internal systems etc? Do we make it clear as to who we expect to make decisions about conflict matters? Are we sure that these duties are not sidelined or delegated? Have we made it clear about the steps we expect to be followed in terms of high-risk scenarios?
Confidentiality and disclosure	This chapter contains the outcomes that must be met if the duty to protect a client's confidential information is to be satisfied. It also includes the interrelated requirements that arise in respect of the duty of disclosure. There is no specific standard stipulating that you have effective systems and controls in place to enable you to identify risks to client confidentiality and to mitigate those risks, but the expectation that this will happen is clear from chapter 2 of the Code for Firms. These are primary duties associated with the role of trusted adviser and the requirements are simple to explain. In practice, this is often a risk danger area and breach risks must be managed and monitored carefully. For example, often the sense of what is required to comply with these outcomes is confused with the conflicts of interest standards; fee earners misunderstand the ethical starting point and/or succumb to client pressures/instructions and place themselves in an unethical, and therefore regulatorily intolerable, position. There are also many external forces at play that may interfere with confidentiality processes (cyber-crime activity etc); plus a breach of confidentiality may also signal a breach of legal duties to protect personal data contained in data protection legislation that applies to the firm and all individuals within it.

continued on next page

Chapter 3: Essential behaviour

Code content	Managerial questions
	Questions for you: Does everyone in the firm understand the all-pervasive and extensive requirements attached to the confidentiality duty? Do our ways of working incorporate strategies to manage risks? Do fee earners understand the need to make a decision about the need to reconcile confidentiality duties with disclosure requirements? Do we have internal policies to address risks attached to use of information barriers?
Court duties	Most of the requirements in most of the chapters in the Codes, and the ethical behaviours they are designed to support, will apply to everyone simply because they are employed in a law firm. The standards which apply in respect of duties to courts (chapters 1 and 2 of the Individual Code and chapters 1 and 7 of the Firm Code) are different in application; they must be met by anyone exercising a right to conduct litigation or acting as an advocate. They explain the twin requirements that arise in respect of duties to the court and duties to the client, and also steer your decision-making in the event that there is a conflict between the interests of each. These standards may be difficult to oversee in management terms; many are directed at the individual in the context of their conduct of litigation and use of the court. However, breaches by individuals may have repercussions for the firm concerned; this may cause scrutiny of the firm's compliance with governance standards in chapter 2 of the Code for Firms and, more widely, attract adverse publicity and have commercial consequences. **Questions for you:** What training do our colleagues need so that our expectations about their duties to the court are understood? What remedies do we have to deal with any pressures or compromises that the client or third parties may inflict on our fee earner?
Introductions to third parties	Again, this may be more limited in application but consideration must be given to whether it is necessary to comply with these standards (described in chapter 5 of the Individual Code and chapter 7 of the Firm Code) that apply only in circumstances where an individual introduces a client to a third party. The ethical expectation is that this will take into account the need to act with integrity, independence, in the client's best interests and as a trusted adviser. It also requires a consideration of the law in this area; particularly in respect of illegal referral fees.

continued on next page

Section 2: Demonstrating regulatory compliance in practice

Code content	Managerial questions
	Questions for you: Have we preferred introducers, do we monitor the introducers for suitability and do we have evidence of the information that we give to clients so that they can make informed decisions?
Publicity	Publicity has a regulatory definition and includes "all promotional material and activity, including the name or description of your firm, stationery, advertisements, brochures, websites, directory entries, media appearances, promotional press releases, and direct approaches to potential clients and other persons, whether conducted in person, in writing, or in electronic form, but does not include press releases prepared on behalf of a client". There are regulatory restrictions that must be met because we are promoting an authorised business or an authorised individual. In addition, there is an overarching duty to understand and comply with advertising legislation. Any unlawful advertising will result in regulatory censure. **Questions for you:** Have we identified and trained those members of the firm who have a marketing role? Have we married this up with duties such as confidentiality? Do we monitor third parties who introduce clients to us?
Regulatory relationships	The standards in chapter 7 of the Individual Code and chapter 3 of the Firm Code strengthen and support the relationship with regulators and ombudsmen. These impose personal duties on individuals within the firm to report and/or cooperate with regulatory enquiries. In practice, proper governance would extend to internal reporting systems to better manage the information channel. **Questions for you:** Do our people understand the regulatory relationship, and do we have internal reporting mechanisms that are understood and used?
Third parties	The need to maintain our role and reputation as trusted advisers is the motivation behind duties to third parties as described in chapter 1 of each of the Codes. The standards may need to be explained to clients who may fail to appreciate that our ethical duties mean that we cannot act in their best interests if this means that we are taking unfair advantage of a third party or misusing our role as an adviser. This extends to ethical duties arising upon the giving or receiving of an undertaking. Again, as with other key

continued on next page

Code content	Managerial questions
	concepts, this is defined for regulatory compliance purposes: "[A] statement, given orally or in writing, whether or not it includes the word 'undertake' or 'undertaking', to someone who reasonably places reliance on it, that you or a third party will do something or cause something to be done, or refrain from doing something." It is essential that the significance of this definition is understood by everyone within the firm as their words may inadvertently create an undertaking that would be binding upon them and the managers. It is essential that solicitors and RELs appreciate that they may in some circumstances give an undertaking that is binding outside the firm environment. Management requirements should extend to managing the risks of such an event occurring in or out of practice. **Questions for you:** Do colleagues understand the behaviours we expect of them? Do they understand the undertaking definition? Do we have an appropriate policy to manage the risks associated with undertakings, and do we have the records to show what undertakings have been given or received?
Separate businesses	Consideration must be given to whether this is relevant. A separate business is a business, wherever situated, that you own, are owned by, actively participate in or are connected with and that is not another SRA-authorised firm, or authorised by another approved regulator, or an overseas or in-house practice. Your connection with a separate business is not unethical provided that certain client protections are applied to the situation and that the separate business does not provide reserved legal activities or immigration services (unless the latter is work that is regulated by the Office of the Immigration Services Commissioner). **Questions for you:** Are we in fact associated with separate businesses and, if so, can we demonstrate that clients of the law firm/customers of the separate business have been given the right information?

Demonstrating compliance with Code behaviours

The Principles, and the Codes of Conduct, ought to cover familiar ground to solicitors. Nevertheless, in their research paper,[30] Vaughan and Oakley report their findings about corporate lawyers' knowledge of the Code. Whilst they are describing the previous rulebook, the sentiments are still pertinent:

> *[C]orporate lawyers cleave to, and know about, these topic-specific rules far more than they cleave to, or know about the 10 underlying, front-end, mandatory principles in the Handbook. This may be of significant concern (in that conduct rules are largely context and point-in-time specific, whereas the principles apply at all times).*

Whilst this may not be what the SRA wants to hear, it is neither a surprising statement nor a situation that is confined to corporate law. However, this does not mean that the law firm manager can be complacent and accept this as the status quo. The challenge of ensuring that the SRA's regulatory requirements are met means that barriers to compliance must be overcome so that a culture is created within the firm where the overarching Principles pervade all decisions made about both client and business topics, and that the relevant Code outcomes are applied in an appropriate manner.

It is essential to have confidence that everyone in the firm understands how they will be expected to react to Code-based requirements.

Consider the standards that everyone, regardless of role or qualification, will be required to achieve:

- client care;
- equality and diversity and inclusion;
- not acting where there is a conflict of interest;
- protecting client information;
- management and supervision duties;
- reporting and notification outcomes;
- duties to third parties; and
- duties relating to the giving or receiving of undertakings.

Specific standards will apply to particular roles. For example, the human resources team must understand the impact of equality and diversity on their role; the litigation lawyers must address the duties arising in respect of duties to the court; and the publicity team must be aware as to the publicity restrictions that are described in the Code for Firms. These must be identified and the firm must be satisfied that members of these teams understand what is expected from them.

In terms of fee earners more generally, it is important that there is confidence that the standards will be interpreted correctly and that systems designed to promote a consistent approach to common issues are not misunderstood. Unfortunately, this is not always the case.

There are many common Code-based conundrums that are often misunderstood and result in difficulties in convincing the regulator to have confidence in the individual and in the firm. Knowing what issues cause confusion could be the basis of tests to evaluate levels of understanding. Consider the following issues that arise in respect of conflicts of interest and confidentiality and disclosure duties:

- duties to former clients – unless a commercial agreement has been concluded, the ethical position is that it is permitted to act against the interests of a former client provided that their confidential information is protected and that you have considered and ruled out an own interest conflict;
- misunderstanding the difference between an ethical duty and a commercial decision;
- not appreciating that a conflict of interest consideration applies only to current clients of the firm; and
- not appreciating that an information barrier does not cure a conflict of interest.

Statement of Solicitor Competence
This is a relatively new and basic knowledge resource that must be understood by all solicitors employed in the firm. Managers should facilitate compliance with this Statement as solicitors are evaluated

against it. The firm should also consider the many best practice reasons for using it as a means to upskill all other employees and enhance the firm's reputation as a good provider of legal services.

The content of the Statement is likely to be less well known than either the Principles- or Codes-based requirements we have already discussed. It was added to the SRA Handbook in 2015 to support the regulator's change from hours-based continuing professional development standards to a system based on the individual solicitor's personal development. This was a significant change and a big clue to the SRA's regulatory expectations.

We are told the following:

For a solicitor, meeting the competences set out in the competence statement forms an integral part of the requirements of service and competence set out in paragraph 3.1 of the Code of Conduct for Solicitors, RELs and RFLs.[31]

So, if competence is defined as being "the ability to perform the roles and tasks required by one's job to the expected standard",[32] then two points should be made:

- The SRA expects to see incremental growth in an individual's competence; and
- competence is not solely tested against knowledge of the law.

In fact, technical knowledge is not a headline feature; instead, it is noteworthy that ethics, professionalism and judgement is the first category of competencies within the document. It is prioritised in the running order above legal knowledge and client relationship skills.

It is important to appreciate that the SRA expects to see these behaviours being demonstrated in practice, and that many relate to the management of the firm.

Such is the importance of the Statement, its terms are reproduced here:

A. *Ethics, professionalism and judgement*
A1. *Act honestly and with integrity, in accordance with legal and*

Chapter 3: Essential behaviour

regulatory requirements and the SRA Standards and Regulations, including
  a Recognising ethical issues and exercising effective judgement in addressing them
  b Understanding and applying the ethical concepts which govern their role and behaviour as a lawyer
  c Identifying the relevant SRA principles and rules of professional conduct and following them
  d Resisting pressure to condone, ignore or commit unethical behaviour
  e Respecting diversity and acting fairly and inclusively

A2. *Maintain the level of competence and legal knowledge needed to practise effectively, taking into account changes in their role and/or practice context and developments in the law, including*
  a Taking responsibility for personal learning and development
  b Reflecting on and learning from practice and learning from other people
  c Accurately evaluating their strengths and limitations in relation to the demands of their work
  d Maintaining an adequate and up-to-date understanding of relevant law, policy and practice
  e Adapting practice to address developments in the delivery of legal services

A3. *Work within the limits of their competence and the supervision which they need, including*
  a Disclosing when work is beyond their personal capability
  b Recognising when they have made mistakes or are experiencing difficulties and taking appropriate action
  c Seeking and making effective use of feedback, guidance and support where needed
  d Knowing when to seek expert advice

A4. *Draw on a sufficient detailed knowledge and understanding of their field(s) of work and role in order to practise effectively, including*

- a Identifying relevant legal principles
- b Applying legal principles to factual issues, so as to produce a solution which best addresses a client's needs and reflects the client's commercial or personal circumstances
- c Spotting issues that are outside their expertise and taking appropriate action, using both an awareness of a broad base of legal knowledge (insofar as relevant to their practice area) and detailed knowledge of their practice area

A5. Apply understanding, critical thinking and analysis to solve problems, including
- a Assessing information to identify key issues and risks
- b Recognising inconsistencies and gaps in information
- c Evaluating the quality and reliability of information
- d Using multiple sources of information to make effective judgements
- e Reaching reasoned decisions supported by relevant evidence

B. Technical legal practice

B1. Obtain relevant facts, including:
- a Obtaining relevant information through effective use of questioning and active listening
- b Finding, analysing and assessing documents to extract relevant information
- c Recognising when additional information is needed
- d Interpreting and evaluating information obtained
- e Recording and presenting information accurately and clearly.

B2. Undertake legal research, including:
- a Recognising when legal research is required
- b Using appropriate methods and resources to undertake the research
- c Identifying, finding and assessing the relevance of sources of law
- d Interpreting, evaluating and applying the results of the research
- e Recording and presenting the findings accurately and clearly.

B3. Develop and advise on relevant options, strategies and solutions, including
- a Understanding and assessing a client's commercial and personal circumstances, their needs, objectives, priorities and constraints
- b Ensuring that advice is informed by appropriate legal and factual analysis and identifies the consequences of different options

B4. Draft documents which are legally effective and accurately reflect the client's instructions including
- a Being able to draft documents from scratch as well as making appropriate use of precedents
- b Addressing all relevant legal and factual issues
- c Complying with appropriate formalities
- d Using clear, accurate and succinct language

B5. Undertake effective spoken and written advocacy2, including
- a Preparing effectively by identifying and mastering relevant facts and legal principles
- b Organising facts to support the argument or position
- c Presenting a reasoned argument in a clear, logical, succinct and persuasive way
- d Making appropriate reference to legal authority
- e Complying with formalities
- f Dealing with witnesses appropriately
- g Responding effectively to questions or opposing arguments
- h Identifying strengths and weaknesses from different parties' perspectives

B6. Negotiate solutions to clients' issues, including
- a Identifying all parties' interests, objectives and limits
- b Developing and formulating best options for meeting parties' objectives
- c Presenting options for compromise persuasively
- d Responding to options presented by the other side
- e Developing compromises between options or parties

B7. Plan, manage and progress legal cases and transactions, including
   a Applying relevant processes and procedures to progress the matter effectively
   b Assessing, communicating and managing risk
   c Bringing the transaction or case to a conclusion

C. Working with other people

C1. Communicate clearly and effectively, orally and in writing, including
   a Ensuring that communication achieves its intended objective
   b Responding to and addressing individual characteristics effectively and sensitively
   c Using the most appropriate method and style of communication for the situation and the recipient(s)
   d Using clear, succinct and accurate language avoiding unnecessary technical terms
   e Using formalities appropriate to the context and purpose of the communication
   f Maintaining the confidentiality and security of communications
   g Imparting any difficult or unwelcome news clearly and sensitively

C2. Establish and maintain effective and professional relations with clients, including
   a Treating clients with courtesy and respect
   b Providing information in a way that clients can understand, taking into account their personal circumstances and any particular vulnerability
   c Understanding and responding effectively to clients' particular needs, objectives, priorities and constraints
   d Identifying and taking reasonable steps to meet the particular service needs of all clients including those in vulnerable circumstances
   e Identifying possible courses of action and their consequences and assisting clients in reaching a decision

    f Managing clients' expectations regarding options, the range of possible outcomes, risk and timescales
    g Agreeing the services that are being provided and a clear basis for charging
    h Explaining the ethical framework within which the solicitor works
    i Informing clients in a timely way of key facts and issues including risks, progress towards objectives, and costs
    j Responding appropriately to clients' concerns and complaints

C3. Establish and maintain effective and professional relations with other people, including
    a Treating others with courtesy and respect
    b Delegating tasks when appropriate to do so
    c Supervising the work of others effectively
    d Keeping colleagues informed of progress of work, including any risks or problems
    e Acknowledging and engaging with others' expertise when appropriate
    f Being supportive of colleagues and offering advice and assistance when required
    g Being clear about expectations
    h Identifying, selecting and, where appropriate, managing external experts or consultants

D. Managing themselves and their own work

D1. Initiate, plan, prioritise and manage work activities and projects to ensure that they are completed efficiently, on time and to an appropriate standard, both in relation to their own work and work that they lead or supervise, including
    a Clarifying instructions so as to agree the scope and objectives of the work
    b Taking into account the availability of resources in initiating work activities

      c Meeting timescales, resource requirements and budgets
      d Monitoring, and keeping other people informed of, progress
      e Dealing effectively with unforeseen circumstances
      f Paying appropriate attention to detail

D2. Keep, use and maintain accurate, complete and clear records, including
      a Making effective use of information management systems (whether electronic or hard copy), including storing and retrieving information
      b Complying with confidentiality, security, data protection and file retention and destruction requirements

D3. Apply good business practice, including
      a Demonstrating an adequate understanding of the commercial, organisational and financial context in which they work and their role in it
      b Understanding the contractual basis on which legal services are provided, including where appropriate how to calculate and manage costs and bill clients
      c Applying the rules of professional conduct to accounting and financial matters
      d Managing available resources and using them efficiently

Other regulatory compliance requirements

We have focused on the three primary sources of behavioural requirements in the SRA Standards and Regulations. Other regulatory standards are also included, and it is necessary to assess other sections for relevance and to develop strategies to demonstrate compliance to the SRA. Evidence of such an assessment with an audit trail to identify compliance responses is a useful internal document.

Chapter 4:
Evidence of compliance

Introduction
The compliance expectation is that you will have responses to the above trust-based standards so that you can provide assurances to the regulator (and sometimes also other stakeholders such as the Legal Ombudsman), as well as your clients and the public at large, that you are delivering legal services in a safe manner and a safe environment.

Not only will you need to have responses, but you will also be expected to have the evidence to support them. In other words, accountability is expected and the means to demonstrate this is an essential part of modern law firm business.

This need for evidence is made clear in the SRA Standards and Regulations, specifically in these places:
- SRA Authorisation of Firms Rules
- SRA Code of Conduct for Solicitors, Registered European Lawyers and Registered Foreign Lawyers, Chapter 7
- SRA Code of Conduct for Firms, Chapter 3

Every authorised entity must plan for the possibility that they might need to have a conversation with their regulator. Any such conversation will be improved by the existence of documented systems, controls and processes.

"Every authorised entity must plan for the possibility that they might need to have a conversation with their regulator. Any such conversation will be improved by the existence of documented systems, controls and processes."

Our problem with this statement is that this may be seen as easier said than done. The SRA gives us very little prescription as to what they expect to see. Instead we are told we must consider what is appropriate for our circumstances, taking into account such factors as the type and size of the business, the firm structure, types of clients and employees, type of work streams and means of delivery and our internal risk analysis work.

Whatever the conclusions about appropriate compliance responses, the firm may struggle to satisfy the SRA that it is achieving regulatory compliance standards in the absence of documentary evidence.

A firm must spend time considering what their evidence will look like. We are talking about an audit trail that includes the following:

- Policies to explain the managerial decisions that have been made about regulatory compliance requirements. These will be placed in the office manual or intranet and will be accessible to all staff. Each policy should include narrative to cover at least the following:
  - a summary of the compliance requirement;
  - the firm's decisions about high-risk or other matters;
  - an explanation as to how individuals must act;
  - details about how to notify risk events (such as a breach of the policy); and
  - internal sources of support.
- Management documentation to explain how the policies will be reviewed to ensure that they remain appropriate and how people will be assessed for compliance with the policies. These documents will perhaps have a more restricted audience than the policies themselves and may be confined to use by the managers, supervisors, human resources etc.
- Documentation relating to the training programmes that are rolled out to support regulatory compliance, together with records of training undertaken by individual employees and the identification of any specific training needs. These documents will be useful to the managers and compliance officers when

assessing their actions against the management and supervision standards in the SRA Codes and also the Statement of Solicitor Competence. Information from them will also be useful to the firm's human resources and learning and development teams.
- Compliance records to demonstrate that all breaches are recorded and considered from the perspective of whether they trigger a notification, with evidence of high-risk issues, enabling the firm to assess its own safety records. Such records ought to be the responsibility of the firm's compliance officers, who will need to share data from them with the managers.
- Risk analysis documents and a risk register. This will be the responsibility of the managers and the compliance officers. The identification of risks, and the explanation about how these will be mitigated, provides the firm with a snapshot of its safety standards.

In terms of the policies that might be contained in an office manual, consider the suggestions in the following non-exhaustive list. Such policies will support the firm in demonstrating that it is aware of required behaviours, as described in the SRA Principles and SRA Codes. The table includes some suggestions as to the risk points that can be answered in the narrative of each policy.

Table 11: Policies for inclusion in the office manual or intranet

Policy	Compliance requirements
Statement about client care policy	Compliance with SRA Principle 7 and SRA Codes standards which apply when acting for members of the public. Do we demonstrate that we have considered whether we can act in a client's best interests, delivered service standard and costs information effectively, been transparent about complaints handling?
Complaints policy	As above.

continued on next page

Policy	Compliance requirements
Equality and diversity policy	SRA Principle 6 and SRA Codes standards as found in chapter 1 of each Code. Do we demonstrate that we encourage equality and diversity in the workplace and toward clients and third parties? Is there a transparent complaints mechanism?
Conflict of interest policy	SRA Principle 7 and SRA Codes standards as found in chapter 6 of each Code. Have we explained to colleagues about the duty to consider own interest conflicts? Have we identified conflicts search requirements and the high-risk scenarios?
Confidentiality policy	SRA Principle 7 and SRA Codes standards as found in chapter 6 of each Code. Have we explained how we will protect confidential information; how decisions will be made about information barriers; what should happen if there is a breach or if a colleague feels that they ought to be disclosing confidential information in the absence of client instructions?
Policy on introductions to third parties	SRA Principles 2, 3 and 5 and SRA Codes standards as found in chapter 5 of the Individual Code and chapter 7 of the Firm Code. Do we have a policy about the protocol? Do we make it clear what information must be given to the client? Do we have methods to vet new arrangements?
Supervision policy	SRA Principles 2, 5 and 7 and SRA Codes standards as found in chapter 3 of the Individual Code and chapter 4 of the Firm Code. Do we explain what we mean by supervision? Is it clear what the role-holder must do?
Outsourcing policy	SRA Principles 2 and 7 plus SRA Code of Conduct for Firms, chapter 2. Do we have a protocol for outsourcing and an explanation about how we will vet new suppliers etc and monitor current arrangements?
Policy on referrals and fee sharing	SRA Principles 2, 3 and 5 and SRA Codes standards as found in chapter 5 of the Individual Code and chapter 7 of the Firm Code. Do we have a policy about the protocol? Do we make it clear what information must be given to the client? Do we have methods to vet new arrangements?
Undertakings policy	SRA Principles 2 and 5 and SRA Codes standards as found in chapter 1 of each Code. Are we clear about who can make undertakings on behalf of the firm? Have we considered the different types of undertaking? Do we have a way of recording all undertakings given or received?

Some final points on policy drafting

Bear in mind the following additional points:

- The examples provided relate to the SRA Codes. There are other parts of the STaRs where compliance will be supported with systems and policies and it is advisable to undertake an assessment exercise to ensure that your audit trail is complete. For example, all firms holding client money must comply with record-keeping as set out in the SRA Accounts Rules, and those performing financial services must consider the evidence needed to demonstrate compliance with the SRA Financial Services (Scope) Rules and SRA Financial Services (Conduct of Business) Rules.

- An important message that must be delivered as part of the compliance strategy is management expectations of all colleagues. For example, everyone must be reminded of their role in supporting the firm's compliance strategy through the use of attendance notes or similar to confirm conversations with clients, as well as internal discussions. Of course, personal diary-keeping is an advisable extra precaution.

Chapter 5:
Safe client inception processes

Introduction

We have already introduced the concept that trust underpins the solicitor–client relationship. This means that in order to be trustworthy, we must understand the regulatory and ethical standards that must be achieved, demonstrated and maintained at all times.

For these reasons, client care is a crucial concept and its complexities must be fully understood. The danger is that this phrase can be interpreted too simply. For example, many practitioners fall into the trap of considering that client care is no more than a need to ensure that they send out client care letters and give proper costs information. They associate client care with service delivery standards. This confusion is compounded by the SRA's use of the phrase in various contexts, in particular to describe the standards of professionalism that relate to dealing with the client's matter, fee arrangements, complaints handling and accepting and refusing instructions.

In fact, the phrase should be interpreted in a more holistic way. If we are to demonstrate that we are trusted advisers, then to care for our clients means that we must provide them with services in a way that meets regulatory expectations and shows our ethical behaviours in practice.

The SRA expects firms to have protective measures in place to ensure that they are indeed considering their clients' needs when providing legal services. This is often described within the firm as client inception, client acceptance or file opening procedures. Again, these phrases can create misunderstandings about the full extent of the consideration. Client inception seems to imply that what we are doing is an administrative or housekeeping function that only needs to be considered at the beginning of a retainer arrangement. It is anything but this.

What follows in this chapter is the identification of the questions that must be considered throughout the client retainer, together with suggestions for a consistent firm-wide approach. Getting any part of the client care process wrong might trigger a number of consequences: disciplinary scrutiny from the regulator in connection with misconduct; the Legal Ombudsman enforcing their powers of enquiry into our services; the displeasure of the client, and more. Poor client care is not good for business.

Client care processes will enable the firm to answer a very simple question: Can we accept instructions to act for a particular client without risking regulatory criticism?

The beginning of the relationship – will it work out?

The initial questions are as follows:
- Have we identified the client correctly? This is not such a strange question; often it is hard to understand the facts presented to you and determine the identity of the client correctly. The SRA Standards and Regulations provides a regulatory definition: the client is "the person for whom you act and, where the context permits, includes prospective and former clients".

    In other words, the client is the person whose interests you are protecting or promoting. Where third parties are involved, it is necessary to establish that they have the client's authority to work with the law firm on the client's behalf.
- Does the client have capacity to instruct the firm? Are the instructions given freely? Does the client display any type of

> *"Client care processes will enable the firm to answer a very simple question: Can we accept instructions to act for a particular client without risking regulatory criticism?"*

Section 2: Demonstrating regulatory compliance in practice

vulnerability that we should account for when providing services? Do we need to adjust the way we deliver our services to meet the needs of this particular client? We must ensure that the client has the correct level of capacity to instruct us. We must not accept instructions if we believe them to be given under duress. These are sometimes difficult judgement calls; capacity calls may involve medical analysis and suggestions of duress must be tackled. Do colleagues have the right support to ensure that these questions are not sidelined? What evidence will the firm want to be added to the file to show why decisions to act, or not act, were made?

- Do we understand what the client wants to achieve and why we have been instructed? Not only does this address retainer issues but it allows us to consider any criminality that may be in the background. Again, we need to have documented conversations as evidence that these issues were tackled.
- Are we satisfied that the client is who they say they are? This addresses both the requirement at paragraph 8.1 in the Code of Conduct for Solicitors, Registered European Lawyers and Registered Foreign Lawyers (and duplicated in the Firm Code), and anti-money laundering legislative requirements in the regulated sector (see Chapter 10). Regardless of this, however, it would be a foolhardy decision not to be satisfied about your client's identity.
- If we are not taking instructions directly from the client, are we confident that instructions provided by someone else have been properly authorised as required in the SRA Codes? What proof will we collect that the client understands how we will proceed and are we satisfied that the third party is entitled to instruct us (either because this is in accordance with the client's freely given wishes or because the third party acts in an appointed position such as an attorney or similar)?
- Does the fee earner or anyone else in the firm involved in the

matter have an own interest conflict, or a significant risk of an own interest conflict, which prevents them from acting for the client? The SRA Codes contain an absolute prohibition on acting in an own interest conflict. Fee earners must take responsibility for declaring such interests.
- Is there a client conflict, or a significant risk of a client conflict, that would mean that the firm must not act? Again, this addresses SRA Codes requirements. It is important that fee earners analyse conflict search results and understand the firm's risk management requirements.
- If a client conflict exists, would we want to use one of the exceptions to the general prohibition and if so, are we able to comply with all necessary conditions attached to the exception? This would raise the risk profile of the matter. The message is that this decision must be made by senior personnel so that any ethical or commercial fallout can be considered.
- Does the fee earner, or anyone involved in the matter, have material information that is relevant to the matter that they cannot reveal because of duties of confidentiality? Again, there are specific ethical requirements. The firm's confidentiality policy should describe the procedural steps and fee earners must understand their responsibilities to be transparent about their concerns.
- Has the retainer been scoped properly? Does the wording of the retainer make any limitations very clear to the client? Would it be straightforward and uncontroversial to justify the limitations to the client, SRA or Ombudsman?
- Are we confident that the client knows what we will, and will not, do?
- Do we have the capacity to provide a proper standard of work? Does the fee earner have the relevant knowledge, time and resources to act competently? Will the fee earner be appropriately supervised?

Fee earners must speak up if they feel that, for whatever reason, they are unable to deliver a proper standard of service.
- Have we considered what information we should give the client about the following matters: likely outcome; the fees, disbursements and any other costs; our expectations of them; what we will be able to do and what we cannot or will not do; our means of communication; and any professional indemnity issues because of the value of the transaction?

  Would anything be a surprise to the client? Do we have the correct documentation to demonstrate what the client was told?
- Would we be breaking the law if we accepted instructions?
- Knowing the client, and the instructions, how risky would it be for the firm to act?

It is a legal requirement that any work placing you under an obligation to comply with the Money Laundering Regulations 2019 (see Chapter 10) is risk assessed in terms of the dangers associated with being used for money laundering purposes. More generally, it is a good preventative measure to risk assess all matters, and this will also often be included on the file opening form.

Such questions as these will usually be collected and completed on a file opening/new matter form/client file front sheet.

This is anything but an administrative exercise. Agreeing to act in a new matter (even in circumstances where this may be a new matter for a well-established client of the firm) is a decision that must be made with a full appreciation of the risks associated with acting illegally or unethically. For this reason, it is important that there is ownership of the decision. Many firms insist that fee earners are responsible for the completion of the file opening form, making clear that they will be required to be accountable for their decision about the risks that have been identified. This requirement should be carefully monitored to ensure that the process is not being delegated to support staff.

The need for continuous monitoring

The risk assessment, and the accuracy of the original information, should be kept under review throughout the retainer. Any changes may alter the relationship with the client and the risk rating of the matter. Again, this oversight, and continuing monitoring, ought to be the responsibility of the fee earner handling the matter. The fee earner's supervisor provides extra oversight and must bear this in mind, and file review and audit processes should include reflection on whether anything has changed that ought to be reflected in an updated front sheet.

Questions that would produce the right ongoing analysis include the following:

- Is the client still the same? As with earlier comments about the client's identity, this is not such a surprising question or unusual position. Client identities will change during the course of retainers for a variety of reasons, some legal and others not, and this requires a reconsideration of all questions relating to checks on identity and purpose of instructions. Are we confident that the change of client makes sense? Have we performed further conflicts checks, considered again the questions arising in respect of confidentiality and disclosure, and repapered our anti-money laundering client due diligence records?
- Despite the initial analysis of the conflict of interest issues, has anything about the matter subsequently altered the initial decision? In other words, have we any information or has anything happened that undermines our confidence in the original decision that it is acceptable to act? Are we still confident that there is not an actual conflict or a significant risk of a conflict?
- Is the scope of the retainer still appropriate? Things change. Has the matter developed in such a way that the terms that were originally agreed with the client are no longer accurate? It is prudent to document any changes.

- Is the original financial information still accurate? Does the starting conversation about fees, disbursements and other costs remain accurate? Have any estimates and agreed financial caps been assessed and are we confident that the former remain accurate and that the latter have not been breached? Any surprises about the costs may generate an internal complaint, Ombudsman interest, and less willingness on the part of the client to settle their account.
- Has the identity of the fee earner or supervisor changed? Has the client been told?
- On reflection, does the client and file risk rating need to be altered?
- Are we still confident that we are not breaking the law or acting unethically?

Client care at the end of the retainer

It is important to understand the concept that client care is not just an exercise to be completed at the beginning of the retainer and does include monitoring for compliance hazards throughout the relationship. However, there is more – what happens at the end of the retainer is equally important.

The client's expectations about their post-retainer relationship with the firm need to be managed to avoid the risk of misunderstandings about what we may, or may not, do in the future. The SRA expects us to keep former clients' information protected and confidential (except where the client gives consent to disclosure or we are legally required to make a disclosure). Data protection legislation defines data processing so that it includes the storage and eventual destruction of personal data.

Any additional agreement with the former client (such as an agreement not to act against them or not to act for their competitors) is a commercial one that is also subject to the ethical and legal duties.

Further analysis as to the compliance requirements is sensible at this stage. The questions below can be used to frame this piece of work:

- Did we achieve what we set out to do? If this did not happen, are the reasons understood by the client?
- Have we explained to the client that the matter has been completed and the nature of our continuing ethical and legal duties?
- If we have agreed any additional commercial agreement with the client, is this clearly expressed and documented? Is the agreement included in our internal policies etc?
- Have we agreed any residual duties such as open undertakings, post completion/settlement matters or retention of funds? Will we ensure that we do not forget to complete these matters? Are we confident that we are acting both lawfully and ethically?
- Has the client been advised about how we will protect their personal data, where and how it will be stored, the period of storage etc?
- Have we accounted to the client in respect of their monies?
- Did anything happen when acting on the matter that will inform any decision about whether to act for the client, or in a particular type of matter, in the future?

"We are legally entitled to perform activities for 'fee, gain or reward' where others would be breaking the law. This heightens the need for trust in what we do as the public have more limited choices."

Chapter 6:
Compliance in the litigation arena

Introduction

There are some obvious reasons why litigation and advocacy are at the more hazardous end of the law firm risk management spectrum:

- Litigation and advocacy are reserved legal activities. We are legally entitled to perform activities for 'fee, gain or reward' where others would be breaking the law. This heightens the need for trust in what we do as the public have more limited choices.
- We have many observers when we perform these activities, not least the judiciary and the press, many of whom have the ear and eye of the SRA. It is not uncommon for the SRA to pursue investigative and disciplinary action on the basis of a judge's comment or a newspaper report. Criticism of behaviours in the court room, or in adversarial matters, will trigger a response because of risk-based regulation and the need to manage potentially harmful publicity about the profession.
- It is more difficult to implement systems and controls to manage risks in this area. Some work streams are more desk-based and procedural and case management systems can be used to ensure appropriate oversight, but this is not the case with all aspects of litigation, particularly at the point where colleagues are using the

court arena for the benefit of their client. How can the firm ensure that this colleague will both know their regulatory and ethical boundaries and act properly?
- There are heightened challenges to the ethical duties of independence and integrity and these are behaviours that the SRA has singled out as being part of its risk priorities.

The regulatory starting point

The regulatory standards that we must achieve in this area are described in the table below.

Table 12: Regulatory expectations in the SRA Standards and Regulations

SRA Standards and Regulations	Regulatory requirement
SRA Principle 1	You act in a way that upholds the constitutional principle of the rule of law, and proper administration of justice.
SRA Principle 2	You act in a way that upholds public trust and confidence in the solicitors' profession and in legal services provided by authorised persons.
SRA Principle 3	You act with independence.
SRA Principle 5	You act with integrity.
SRA Code of Conduct for Solicitors, RELs and RFLs, paragraph 1.4; SRA Code of Conduct for Firms, paragraph 1.4	You do not mislead or attempt to mislead your clients, the court or others, either by your own acts or omissions or by allowing or being complicit in the acts or omissions of others (including your client).
SRA Code of Conduct for Solicitors etc, paragraph 2.1; SRA Code of Conduct for Firms, paragraph 7.1(a)	You do not misuse or tamper with evidence or attempt to do so.
SRA Code of Conduct for Solicitors etc, paragraph 2.2; SRA Code of Conduct for Firms, paragraph 7.1(a)	You do not seek to influence the substance of evidence, including generating false evidence or persuading witnesses to change their evidence.

continued on next page

Chapter 6: Compliance in the litigation arena

SRA Standards and Regulations	Regulatory requirement
SRA Code of Conduct for Solicitors etc, paragraph 2.3; SRA Code of Conduct for Firms, paragraph 7.1(a)	You do not provide or offer to provide any benefit to witnesses dependent upon the nature of their evidence or the outcome of the case.
SRA Code of Conduct for Solicitors etc, paragraph 2.4; SRA Code of Conduct for Firms, paragraph 7.1(a)	You only make assertions or put forward statements, representations or submissions to the court or others which are properly arguable.
SRA Code of Conduct for Solicitors etc, paragraph 2.5; SRA Code of Conduct for Firms, paragraph 7.1(a)	You do not place yourself in contempt of court, and you comply with court orders which place obligations on you.
SRA Code of Conduct for Solicitors etc, paragraph 2.6; SRA Code of Conduct for Firms, paragraph 7.1(a)	You do not waste the court's time.
SRA Code of Conduct for Solicitors etc, paragraph 2.7; SRA Code of Conduct for Firms, paragraph 7.1(a)	You draw the court's attention to relevant cases and statutory provisions, or procedural irregularities of which you are aware, and which are likely to have a material effect on the outcome of the proceedings.

The table includes both ethical duties and regulatory standards that must be met by litigators and advocates. The clear message is that a lawyer's primary motivation is to show that they use court processes properly.

Ordinarily, this ought to be compatible with the duty to act in a client's best interests, but where this balance cannot be achieved it is the duty to the court that takes precedence. Such is the importance of correctly understanding the position, it is made clear by the introduction to the SRA Principles which includes the following statement:

You should, where relevant, inform your client of the circumstances in which your duty to the Court and other professional obligations will outweigh your duty to them.

In practice, and with some clients and matters, this may be difficult to achieve. Law firm managers must be satisfied that colleagues – particularly perhaps those who are less experienced – understand that it is sometimes necessary not to act on client instructions. Has this message been given to colleagues? Is this behaviour supervised?

Section 2: Demonstrating regulatory compliance in practice

In more detail: independence and integrity in practice

Such are the importance of these two ethically based behaviours to the topics of proper governance, risk management and compliance with regulatory standards and legal duties, that the more detailed analysis of their meaning could in fact be placed anywhere in this book.

The fact that this analysis is included within our discussion about litigation should not create an impression that this is the only work stream where these topics must be considered. On the contrary, independence and integrity must pervade every decision that is made and every action taken by all members of the firm.

Litigation is a pinch point in terms of reconciling personal duties with duties to the client. These behaviours must be evidenced in practice. Where this does not happen, the failure inevitably attracts judicial criticism and journalistic attention and/or SRA interest and enforcement action.

The SRA has included lack of integrity in its Risk Outlook, and placed emphasis on litigation (highlighting personal injury, payment protection insurance and holiday sickness work) as a cause for concern. It explains why this is so as follows:

> Acting without integrity and independence in litigation can lead to poor outcomes, which undermines the proper administration of justice. As their trusted adviser, solicitors owe duties to their client, but they also owe duties to third parties, the court and the wider public interest.[33]

Law firm managers must ensure that colleagues understand the behaviours they are expected to demonstrate in practice, and these must be monitored.

The meaning of 'independence'

SRA Principle 3 simply states, "You act with independence", providing further commentary on the meaning of this in practice elsewhere in the STaRs.[34]

continued on page 139

AN INSIDER'S INSIGHT

The following article is contributed by John Whitehouse. John is a solicitor who has worked for the SRA as a senior ethics adviser and is an ethics and compliance specialist. Here, he shares an interesting commentary which provides answers to why this is a priority behaviour which must be demonstrated by individuals and which must be facilitated through the firm's compliance culture.

When you mention the word independence, most lawyers will think about giving independent advice and avoiding a conflict of interest. This is correct, but there is a broader application of Principle 3 of the SRA Principles 2019, which states that you must act with independence. This Principle applies to both individuals and firms. In this section we will define what we mean by independence and refer to the relevant parts of the SRA Standards and Regulations which will help you embed the Principle in your practice and procedures. This overview of what it means to be independent is passing on my experience in both advising lawyers and carrying out regulatory investigations, and is written to help you comply with your professional duties.

Defining independence

There is no definition of independence given in the revised SRA Principles, although the one given in the previous SRA Handbook is indicative of its broad application:

> 'Independence' means your own and your firm's independence, and not merely your ability to give independent advice to a client. You should avoid situations which might put your independence at risk – eg, giving control of your practice to a third party which is beyond the regulatory reach of the SRA or other approved regulator.

Although the previous SRA Handbook has been replaced, there is no indication of an intention to change the substance of the definition of independence.

Section 2: Demonstrating regulatory compliance in practice

Relevant sections of the SRA Standards and Regulations

The SRA Standards and Regulations cover four main areas where the independence Principle is particularly relevant:

- *refusing to act where your own interests, or your firm's interests, conflict with the client's interests;*[35]
- *not acting for two or more clients when you cannot act in each client's best interests;*[36]
- *not allowing a third-party introducer to influence how you run your firm or give advice to the client;*[37] *and*
- *retaining your independence in court proceedings.*[38]

Firms are required to have procedures in place to achieve and comply with the Principles and other requirements in the SRA Standards and Regulations. Procedures must be written down and be easily accessible by employees. Firms must also identify, manage and monitor their risks,[39] *which would include any potential compliance issues relating to the SRA Principles. Partners and key staff must be aware of the risks recorded in the firm's risk register.*

One of the main procedures a firm will have is in relation to avoiding conflicts of interest. Your procedure should include how you record your decisions. For example, if you are considering acting for both a buyer and seller in a property transaction, the record should include the factors that were considered in arriving at a decision. In practical terms, you need to demonstrate compliance, should any question be raised by a client or the SRA.

To ensure independence of a practice, solicitors and other regulated persons must only practise in ways permitted by both the SRA Authorisation of Firms Rules and the SRA Authorisation of Individuals Rules. This means that for a recognised body all of the owners and managers must be solicitors, or other approved categories of lawyer.[40] *Third party non-lawyer ownership is not permitted, except where the firm is licensed by the SRA (or other designated regulator) as an Alternative Business Structure.*[41] *An unregulated third party acquiring an option to purchase a law firm for a nominal fee would not be in compliance with the independence Principle.*

Situations when your independence may be compromised

While most solicitors who find themselves before the Solicitors Disciplinary Tribunal are alleged to have been dishonest or have committed a serious breach of the SRA Accounts Rules, there are some decisions relating to independence which confirm the importance of achieving this key Principle.

Referral arrangements

The operation of a compensation scheme for miners who had contracted diseases from working practices gave rise to disciplinary cases, when solicitors had failed to act with independence. In particular, concerns were expressed by the tribunal about relationships with introducers of work:

> [B]y entering into the agreement with Justice Direct [the introducer], the Respondent effectively disabled himself from advising clients as to the desirability of the client becoming liable to pay 25% of any recoverable damages to Justice Direct in return for an introduction to the solicitor [...] the solicitor was facilitating the imposition on the client of an agreement which [...] By so doing the solicitor's independence and integrity were impaired.[42]

In another case the tribunal was concerned about the firm receiving a substantial amount of work from one source and the effect of this on the solicitor's independence. The failure to advise clients on the agreement they had entered into with the introducer was a "culpable failure" and "The Tribunal considered that the Respondent ran the risk of compromising her independence because if she had advised clients against the UGS [introducer] agreement she might well not have received any more referrals from that source."[43]

If you accept referrals from an introducer, you will need to carefully check the relevant paragraphs of the SRA Codes of Conduct. One important question to ask yourself is, "Is the introducer directing me, or the client, as to how the case must proceed?" If the answer is yes, then you may be at risk of breaching the independence Principle. If the introducer is a legal expenses insurer, or other funder, then there may be legitimate constraints on how the client may give instructions.

Litigation

In 2017 allegations were made against Philip Shiner that at a press conference, he personally endorsed his clients' allegations that the British Army had unlawfully killed and tortured Iraqi civilians. In respect of this allegation the tribunal found, "By associating himself with the allegations, without having taken steps to be absolutely certain of their veracity, he had allowed his independence to be compromised."[44]

In conclusion, whether you are a fee earner or Partner in a firm, you will need to understand the independence Principle, how it relates to individual client cases, how the practice is structured and the type of business arrangements your firm is permitted to enter. While not allowing your independence to be compromised is important in each case, the way your business is structured and arrangements with third parties for referrals present a potentially greater risk. Many lawyers have been enticed by the prospect of referrals from an introducer, who may want to retain control of the client's case, or have access to their damages. Therefore, referral arrangements must be checked carefully.

One simple and practical way to check whether you are acting with independence is to ask an experienced colleague who has no connection with the matter in hand. Situations that occur in practice will often need careful analysis, with the assistance of your firm's compliance officer, or from a specialist adviser.

continued from page 134

The meaning of 'integrity'

SRA Principle 5 states as follows: "You act with integrity."

Ask any group of people to describe what integrity means to them, and inevitably you will receive a number of different explanations. It is an interesting interview question and well worth asking. It is a characteristic that must be displayed by all colleagues. The firm's compliance culture and even its authorised status may be put in jeopardy by just one individual's actions, so an understanding of their views on this requirement is insightful.

Asking what integrity means to a colleague is not flippant. The SRA has chosen not to insert a definition of the term into the SRA Standards and Regulations. The SRA has produced separate guidance to explain its position on lack of integrity. Please note the following:

Cases where we are likely to take disciplinary action for lack of integrity:
- *Where there has been a wilful or reckless disregard of standards, rules, legal requirements and obligations or ethics, including an indifference to what the applicable provisions are or to the impacts or consequences of a breach.*
- *Where the regulated firm or individual has taken unfair advantage of clients or third parties or allowed others to do so.*
- *Where the regulated firm or individual has knowingly or recklessly caused harm or distress to another.*
- *Where clients or third parties have been misled or allowed to be misled (except where this is a result of simple error that the regulated firm or individual has corrected as soon as they became aware of it).*[45]

Notwithstanding this vagueness, the SRA has used this behaviour as a test by which individual solicitors are judged in terms of their suitability to remain as members of the profession. Many solicitors have been removed from the roll on the basis of the SDT's evaluation that they lack integrity, and have appealed these career-ending decisions on the basis of the interpretation applied to this Principle.

Integrity is a current regulatory risk priority and the SRA is clear and unequivocal in stating that it will take enforcement action against individuals where this is in the public interest. This has led to a number of thought-provoking decisions in the SDT that develop our understanding, not so much about what integrity is, but rather about what the SRA regards as a lack of integrity that allows an individual's ability to remain in the profession to be put to test.

Consider the following example of an SDT judgment on an agreed outcome between the SRA and a solicitor, Amanda Davies.[46] Ms Davies agreed to be struck off the roll because of conduct issues related to the backdating of 23 letters on clinical negligence and personal injury cases. She also admitted to making misleading statements to the mother of a client bringing a claim following the death of her husband in a road traffic accident. Ms Davies told the SRA that she had wanted to show her supervisors that she was in control of her caseload and that her files were progressing, and said that it was "simply a case that I was no longer able to cope" and was attempting "to give myself some breathing space" in dealing with files. In the SDT's judgment, Ms Davies was held to have breached the duty of integrity, as well as the duty to uphold trust and confidence in the profession; and was alleged to have been dishonest.

AN INSIDER'S INSIGHT

Some further clarity as to the meaning of integrity, and the SDT and case law that have developed our understanding of this behaviour, is provided in the following article written by **Katherine Galza**, an associate solicitor with Kingsley Napley LLP. The article was published on the firm's website in March 2018,[47] and is reproduced here with their kind permission. It represents an invaluable insight into regulatory and legal thinking, and the examples provided are helpful for anyone involved in law firm and risk management, allowing them to consider whether any acts that have been tested against the integrity value could occur in their own business.

The quality of integrity: A review of the Court of Appeal's decision in Wingate and Evans v SRA; SRA v Malins *in the context of legal services regulation*
Shockwaves (at least within the professional discipline world) followed

the recent decision in Malins v SRA[48] *as the very existence of a 'lack of integrity' offence hung in the balance. A break with tradition was, however, short-lived and the combined appeal of* Wingate and Evans v SRA *and* SRA v Malins[49] *has now restored much of the status quo. But what is this nebulous concept of 'integrity' in the context of the SRA's Code of Conduct? What does it mean for solicitors, barristers and legal executives trying to uphold it?*

Background

In the above case, the Court of Appeal considered two separate appeals, both linked to the meaning of integrity and dishonesty. Wingate and Evans, *in short, involved a partner of a law firm signing a loan agreement, knowing that he could not meet the terms of the contract and assuming that it would be superseded by another version that had been agreed orally. At first instance, the SDT found that signing the 'sham' funding agreement amounted to a lack of integrity, a concept that involved only one objective test. The Respondents unsuccessfully appealed this decision in the High Court.*

Similarly, Malins *involved a partner backdating a letter and sending it to the other side in order to recover an ATE premium where the original form had been lost. A finding by the SDT against Mr Malins was subsequently overturned by the High Court, which held that dishonesty and lack of integrity were synonymous, and that the SRA's failure to plead dishonesty in the first instance meant that the matter needed to be re-tried.*

The cases were listed together in the Court of Appeal, which enabled the Court to conclude definitively that, although linked, 'lack of integrity' did not equate to dishonesty.

Integrity defined

Lord Jackson's judgment reviewed a historic catalogue of cases touching on the meaning of integrity and how it could be distinguished from dishonesty. He cited Newell-Austin v Solicitors Regulation Authority,[50] *in which integrity amounted to "moral soundness, rectitude and steady* adherence to an ethical code". Bolton v Law Society,[51] also cited, went further, with Sir Bingham MR arguing as follows:

> Any solicitor who is shown to have discharged his professional duties with anything less than complete integrity, probity and trustworthiness must expect severe sanctions to be imposed upon him by the Solicitors Disciplinary Tribunal.

Indeed, this idea that solicitors (and by extension, barristers and legal executives) should be held to an additional yet distinct ethical standard tied directly to the nature and the practicalities of their work formed the basis of Jackson's own analysis. It should be noted, however, that he tempered this view with the assertion that "[t]he duty of integrity does not require professional people to be paragons of virtue".

Where Jackson considered honesty to be "a basic moral quality which is expected of all members of society", integrity was "a useful shorthand to express the higher standards which society expects from professional persons and which the professions expect from their own members". Therefore, dishonesty was simply an "aggravating feature", rather than a discrete offence under the Code. In the context of Malins' backdated letter, the act of creating the letter demonstrated a lack of integrity, but it was by virtue of the letter being sent to the other party that the aggravating element of dishonesty was added to the mix.

What does this mean for legal professionals?

In the main, Jackson's ruling restores the traditional interpretation of "a lack of integrity" pre-Malins. It is, however, worth noting that he refrained from any comment concerning the case of Bar Standards Board v Howd,[52] in which the court found that "inappropriate and offensive social or sexual behaviour" was not relevant to professional integrity. As such, it will be interesting to see if this position remains unchallenged as #MeToo spreads to the legal profession (see The Lawyer's recent survey on sexual harassment in law).[53]

The case also highlights a few practical points for legal professionals that are summarised below.

- *First, Jackson's review of the relevant cases is a helpful summary, identifying types of behaviour that amount to "a lack of integrity". These are as follows:*
  - *a sole practice giving the appearance of being a partnership and deliberately flouting the conduct rules (*Emeana*);*
  - *recklessly, but not dishonestly, allowing a court to be misled (*Brett*);*
  - *subordinating the interests of the clients to the solicitors' own financial interests (*Chan*);*
  - *making improper payments out of the client account (*Scott*);*
  - *allowing the firm to become involved in conveyancing transactions that bear the hallmarks of mortgage fraud (*Newell-Austin*); and*
  - *making false representations on behalf of the client (*Williams*).*
- *Second, solicitors, barristers and other legal professionals conducting negotiations or making representations in court (for example) are expected to be "even more scrupulous about accuracy than a member of the general public in daily discourse".*
- *Third, acts that demonstrate a lack of integrity can also amount to "manifest incompetence" so as to fall foul of Principle 6 of the SRA Code ("you must: ... behave in a way that maintains the trust the public places in you and in the provision of legal services").*[54]
- *Fourth, medical evidence is unlikely to exculpate an act that lacks integrity, although it can be used in mitigation to explain how the Respondent interacted with the SRA during the disciplinary proceedings. Moreover, previous good character, according to Mr Justice Holman, "can do little to mitigate the seriousness of misconduct or the sanction that must follow".*
- *Fifth, in stating that a professional disciplinary tribunal (as compared to a jury "drawn from the wider community") has "specialist knowledge of the profession to which the respondent belongs and of the ethical standards of that profession", Jackson*

argued that "[t]he decisions of such a body must be respected, unless it has erred in law". It can therefore be construed that a disciplinary tribunal's decision as to what amounts to lack of integrity within the profession will be given considerably more weight than the verdict of a jury or any other judicial panel.

Conclusion
The quality of integrity is no longer strained. Dishonesty is no longer a synonym, and no longer needs to be pleaded by the SRA in order to bring home an allegation under Principle 2 of the SRA Rules.[55] Fundamentally, legal professionals are reminded of their distinct positioning in the regulatory world and are encouraged to think whether their actions, though honest, might contravene a higher standard of professionalism.

Risk pinch points in litigation and strategies to manage them
Such is the regulator's concern that we uphold the rule of law and act ethically in court proceedings that it has produced a number of documents setting out its position, with which it expects us to be familiar.

These include warning notices and risk publications. Law firm managers and compliance officers will want to ensure that they are aware of all new publications and can demonstrate that, where appropriate, they are used to improve the internal risk management response.

Regarding litigation, we are given the following resources:
- Warning notice – Risk Factors in Personal Injury Claims[56]

    This notice contains a commentary on the risks associated with this type of work which the SRA considers intolerable, and in respect of which we are expected to manage and mitigate risk events.

    These events include issues arising in respect of cold calling, referral arrangements, third-party instructions, clients' interests, bogus identity issues, misunderstandings about costs, and accounting to the client.

We are told that we are expected to demonstrate adequate oversight of staff training and office systems so that, for example, we have evidence of the following as described in the warning notice:
- well-trained staff who are in a position to offer a proper standard of service to clients;
- systems to ensure that matters are triaged effectively by those who have experience in and an understanding of the litigation process;
- systems that allow for the diarising of limitation periods and court timetables;
- staff training that is reviewed regularly to ensure that skills and knowledge are updated; and
- full and proper supervision of staff where work is overseen, and support and further expertise is available to fee earners and case workers.

We are also advised as to the risks of taking on files from another firm without due diligence on the files and a consideration of whether we have the necessary competence (in the form of time, resources and experience) to act in the client's best interests.

Bear in mind that the SRA makes it clear that failure to have proper regard to warning notices is likely to lead to disciplinary action.

The full suite of warning notices is collated on the SRA website.[57] Other warning notices that are particularly important documents in the litigation department are as follows:
- holiday sickness claims;
- PPI claims;
- referral fees, LASPO and SRA Principles; and
- bogus law firms and identity theft.
• SRA Risk Resource Report – Walking the line: the balancing of duties in litigation[58]

This is essential reading if the risks of providing litigation and advocacy services are to be managed appropriately. The report identifies some challenges to acting properly and examines the ways in which misconduct can arise. Again, the regulatory starting point is that we must not compromise or justify our decisions on the basis of acting in a client's best interests.

The SRA expresses this sentiment in this way:

Although solicitors must fearlessly advance their clients' cases, they are not "hired guns" whose only duty is to their client. They also owe duties to the courts, third parties and to the public interest. Breach of those duties can give rise, for example, to wasted costs orders or to findings of misconduct.

Examples are given where the SRA considers that a solicitor may be prioritising their client's interests in an inappropriate way and, in so doing, running the risk of acting unethically. We are given the following scenarios:

- predatory litigation against third parties (ie, litigation is threatened to obtain settlement in cases that have little or no merit);
- abuse of the litigation process whereby the solicitor uses litigation or advocacy rights for purposes not directly connected to resolving a particular matter;
- taking unfair advantage of a third party;
- misleading the court; or
- pursuing excessive or aggressive litigation at the client's request.

The SRA also gives examples where it considers that the solicitor fails to act in their client's best interests, such as in the following scenarios:

- predatory litigation where clients are encouraged to proceed with litigation where their case has little or no merit or where litigation is unnecessary; or
- taking on weak or unwinnable costs without making the risks (costs and other risks) known to the client.

Chapter 7:
Adding the people and commercial perspective to regulatory standards

Introduction
Achieving regulatory compliance standards is a mission that must not be compromised. A firm may employ very good lawyers but still find itself under regulatory scrutiny if those individuals do not demonstrate the right ethical attributes when delivering services. Equally, a poorly run firm will attract regulatory attention if there is no acknowledgement of the role of the SRA in the firm's internal management.

We have already highlighted the basic knowledge requirements, various compliance strategies, and tensions that may arise where client care responses are inappropriate or where litigation services are being performed. What underpins all these topics is the need for the correct response to the compliance role from people, specifically from people we work with in the business and people outside and to whom we provide legal services.

Communicating the correct messages to colleagues
The best-planned strategies, and the most beautifully crafted policies, will not be good enough to withstand regulatory oversight unless there is confidence that the people within the firm are compliant in practice.

The commercial benefits of an ethical service

You may work with individuals who are critical of the firm's focus on regulation, compliance and ethics. We have already discussed the need to incorporate into the management processes the risks attached to their unwillingness to act in a safe way.

Their point of view can perhaps be understood, although of course it must never be tolerated or allowed to gain any credence. A maverick's perspective will be based on the concept that the need to think about compliance and ethics somehow obstructs their role in the firm which is to provide legal services and make money for the business. They see compliance in a negative way distracting them from their "day job" and complicating the real purpose of the firm.

Consider the standards in chapter 2 of the SRA Code of Conduct for Firms and the need for financial risk management. This implicitly requires a consideration of how to run a profitable business; not because this is a regulatory objective in itself but because the regulator considers that a financially viable firm is more likely to be a trustworthy firm that is beneficial to clients and the public at large. Critics will believe that this is unnecessary oversight that serves no purpose, but the regulator requires this oversight as necessary since it regulates in the public interest and with consumer protection objectives in mind.

There is more to these topics than this. Early, or more willing, adopters of risk-based regulation understand the benefits that demonstrating compliance and ethics can have for the business. Most clients want to instruct well-run and ethical law firms, so this is a selling point to those cynics within your framework. And not only is ethics good for clients, it is good to work within an ethical environment where an individual can be assured that they will be supported in making the right choices for themselves as well as for the clients, and where mavericks are more uncomfortable.

In other words, compliance and ethics are good for business. This is a widely held regulatory position. Consider the following commentary from the Law Society of New South Wales:

The Law Society seeks to align the commercial imperatives that drive the business of legal practice with the regulatory framework ... This approach encourages solicitors to view regulatory compliance, not as an authoritative burden, but as a means to generate client satisfaction and drive profitability.[59]

This is a premise with growing kudos. Increasingly, compliance and ethics are qualities that progressive law firms are promoting to win and retain clients.

AN INSIDER'S INSIGHT

Our next contribution from a thought leader is by **Iain Miller** who is a partner at Kingsley Napley LLP. He specialises in legal services regulation and legal ethics. He is the General Editor of *Cordery on Legal Services* and writes extensively on the regulation of law firms. Iain's views are persuasive and can be used to convince disbelievers of the benefits of working in an ethical way.

In England and Wales, we are out of step with most other common law jurisdictions in that in both education and practice we do not place any great emphasis on legal ethics. That does not mean we are unethical. What it does mean is that we have for many years adopted the language and approach of compliance and risk in dealing with both individual and law firm management. In contrast, in the US, Australia and Canada, legal ethics is very much at the centre of legal training and also how law firms approach their internal regulation. It is only in recent years that those jurisdictions have begun to look at compliance-based regulation, mainly as a useful tool to deploy in relation to entity regulation.[60]

It seems that in law firms within England and Wales the idea of promoting legal ethics, let alone aligning the firm's values and objectives around legal ethics, is viewed without much enthusiasm. It is nice to have, but cannot really compete for time, or budget, with AML issues or the onslaught of the GDPR. That is before we move on to the risks of cyber security.

Whilst this might explain the collective lack of enthusiasm for legal ethics, a law firm that embraces legal ethics is more likely to survive and prosper in the coming years and decades. The cause of this will be the looming upheaval in legal services brought about by the advancement of technology, coupled with a shift in society's view of what is acceptable business practice.

Legal ethics at its heart is based on the premise that in a free society the practice of law has a moral purpose. It enables clients' rights to be protected by a lawyer who fearlessly advocates those rights. However, the duty of a lawyer to act in their client's best interest is tempered by that lawyer's duties to the court to ensure that justice is administered fairly and in the interests of wider society. This was succinctly expressed by Lord Neuberger in the 2012 Upjohn Lecture:

> This leads me directly to the question of the purpose of the legal profession. A vibrant, independent legal profession is an essential element of any democratic society committed to the rule of law. It is not merely another form of business, solely aimed at maximising profit whilst providing a competitive service to consumers. I am far from suggesting that lawyers ought not seek to maximise their profits, or ought not provide a competitive service. What I am saying is that lawyers also owe overriding specific duties to the court and to society, duties that go beyond the maximisation of profit and that may require lawyers to act to their own detriment, and to that of their clients.[61]

The existence of rules governing lawyers' conduct and practice is a strategy for giving effect to these principles. Complying with the rules will assist lawyers in achieving the ethical purpose.

The wider concept of the lawyer or law firm in society also needs to be seen alongside an increasing emphasis on businesses more generally behaving ethically. Following on from the banking crisis there is a sense that we need to encourage businesses to be mindful of their role in *society rather than operating purely for personal or corporate interests.*

Professor Christopher Hodges of Oxford University described this wider purpose as follows:[62]

The essence of a modern democracy is based on respect for others, expressed through support for fundamental human rights. Applying that political policy to a vibrant market economy produces the result that society supports mutual exchange through honest trade so as to improve the common good. Trade and harmonious society function on the basis of trust. So the purpose of regulation of business activity is to enable widespread trust in traders, on the basis of which a healthy, sustainable and growing economy can exist, which in turn supports employment, social stability and innovation.

One can easily see how the concept of legal ethics fits very well into this overarching economic model of ethical businesses serving the greater needs of society.

This renewed interest in ethical business sits alongside technological advances in relation to the practice of law. It is clear that technology is enabling in-house legal teams to be more efficient and reduce the work that they outsource. At the same time areas such as contract review, disclosure and research are being increasingly driven by technology. No one knows how this will exactly play out. It may well be that a law firm in 10 or so years' time will be similar in structure to a high end consultancy. It will have fewer staff than current firms. This because there will no longer be the work to sustain the current leverage model.[63] *It will provide expert advice based on experience in relation to those issues that clients consider high risk or high value. In doing so, it will rely upon and use the services of a variety of legal technology companies to provide services such as document analysis and research.*

The continued existence of the law firm model will rely on its ability to provide a service that clients can choose to pay for over and above the technology itself. Law will be a discretionary purchase as the institutions such as the land registry and the courts will be fully accessible directly by clients through blockchain and other technologies. Consequently, there will be fewer law firms than exist at present. The prospect of this change creates existential issues for law firms. Those that do survive will need to have a strong ethical culture.

The concept of law firms being broadly ethical is not a new one and these days it often sits under the umbrella of corporate social responsibility. Many law firms readily participate in a number of programmes that demonstrate public good. These involve pro bono work, charitable work, encouraging diversity and inclusion and reducing the environmental impact of firms' work. It is odd that firms usually stop short of any formal programme around legal ethics that directly addresses the public good of lawyers in society irrespective of whether they recycle more paper than the next firm. This may result from a sense that clients want a firm that will fight on their behalf and ethics sends the wrong message. However, the value of the law firm of the future will be the ability to keep clients out of trouble. Clients will want advice from someone with a well-developed moral compass. Otherwise short-term victories brought about by aggressive tactics will become, in the longer term, damaging headlines and reputational loss. In addition, as it becomes more important for businesses themselves to behave ethically they will seek out law firms that share their values.

The sooner law firms start to think about demonstrating their ethical credentials the better adapted they will be.

Chapter 8:
The Legal Ombudsman – why are we bothered?

Introduction

Many lawyers will recall the previous form of regulation of solicitors and law firms and the many different roles of the Law Society of England and Wales. This body was a one-stop shop acting as the regulator of the profession, the representative body of the profession, and the investigator of service complaints brought by clients against solicitors and law firms. Complaints were handled by a division of the Law Society which many practitioners will recognise by the title of Office for the Supervision of Solicitors, but latterly was described as the Legal Complaints Service.

Move forward to the current style of regulation introduced with the Legal Services Act 2007, and neither the Law Society nor the SRA have the right to investigate service complaints. Instead, this is a role given to an independent, statutorily created body known as the Office for Legal Complaints (OLC). The OLC is the board of the Legal Ombudsman (LeO), also established by the 2007 Act.

LeO has the responsibility to investigate complaints about all legal service providers and claims management companies in England and Wales. The office is independent and answerable to the Legal Services Board. It must uphold the regulatory objectives in the Legal Services Act and does this most explicitly through protecting consumers.

Section 2: Demonstrating regulatory compliance in practice

The majority of its investigations arise in respect of the services provided by solicitors and SRA-authorised firms. This is not alarming and is explained by the fact that this is the largest part of the legal services industry. A number of remedies are available if LeO considers that a service provider is at fault. LeO can order the refund or reduction of fees or the payment of compensation, insist that extra work is needed to put things right, insist that we apologise for our actions, and order us to return documents.

The matters that are investigated by LeO may also unearth conduct issues. It is not part of LeO's role to investigate misconduct, and concerns will be referred to the SRA for investigation.

The connection between LeO and the SRA

So, does the Legal Ombudsman matter? The answer is a resounding yes. Not only does this body have the right to take action against solicitors and law firms, it is another source of intelligence for the SRA, giving the latter valuable information about whether it ought to have concerns about the authorised status of the individual or the law firm.

This means that law firm strategy must extend to managing the risk of being the subject of an enquiry by the Legal Ombudsman. The worst case outcome of such an enquiry is the imposition of an order on the firm to do, or not do, something and/or a referral to the SRA. The best case outcome is still a distraction as any investigation will divert the firm's resources.

The SRA sets out its expectations about the relationship we must have with LeO in the SRA Standards and Regulations. Consider these personal duties for solicitors and other directly regulated lawyers in the Code of Conduct for Solicitors, RELs and RFLs in chapter 7:

- 7.3: *You cooperate with the SRA, other regulators, ombudsmen, and those bodies with a role overseeing and supervising the delivery of, or investigating concerns in relation to, legal services.*
- 7.5: *You do not attempt to prevent anyone from providing*

information to the SRA or any other body exercising regulatory, supervisory, investigatory or prosecutory functions in the public interest.

These duties are duplicated in chapter 3 of the SRA Code of Conduct for Firms to ensure that there is firm-wide compliance.

It is therefore important to acknowledge the symbiotic relationship between these two oversight bodies; ultimately, they have a common purpose which is to ensure consumer and public confidence in the regulated legal services market. They often work together and, for example, commission joint research projects to improve their understanding of risk matters.

Strategies to manage LeO's interest in your business

LeO has the right to investigate client service complaints only in circumstances where the firm's internal complaints handling process has proved unsuccessful and the client (and in some cases, also a prospective client) remains unsatisfied.

This position triggers the need to consider various points that a good law firm will incorporate into its compliance culture to manage the relationship.

Consider the following:

- The firm must be confident that it can deliver services in the manner agreed with the client. This requires a common understanding about the importance of giving proper and true information to the client about the level of service, means of communication, limitations, costs and similar.
- The firm must have an effective complaints procedure intended to address and remedy issues without the need for LeO involvement. This requires an understanding of the meaning of a complaint. 'Complaint' is not a defined term in the SRA Standards and Regulations, but was defined for regulatory purposes in the previous SRA Handbook as follows:

> [A]n oral or written expression of dissatisfaction which alleges that the complainant has suffered (or may suffer) financial loss, distress, inconvenience or other detriment.

- The firm must have a response to regulatory requirements about complaints handling as expressed in the standards in chapter 8 of the SRA Code of Conduct for Solicitors, RELs and RFLs (which are duplicated in the SRA Code of Conduct for Firms):

  > 8.2: *You ensure that, as appropriate in the circumstances, you either establish and maintain, or participate in, a procedure for handling complaints in relation to the legal services you provide.*
  >
  > 8.3: *You ensure that clients are informed in writing at the time of engagement about:*
  >
  > *(a) their right to complain to you about your services and your charges;*
  >
  > *(b) how a complaint can be made and to whom; and*
  >
  > *(c) any right they have to make a complaint to the Legal Ombudsman and when they can make any such complaint.*
  >
  > 8.4: *You ensure that when clients have made a complaint to you, if this has not been resolved to the client's satisfaction within 8 weeks following the making of a complaint they are informed, in writing:*
  >
  > *(a) of any right they have to complain to the Legal Ombudsman, the time frame for doing so and full details of how to contact the Legal Ombudsman; and*
  >
  > *(b) if a complaint has been brought and your complaints procedure has been exhausted:*
  >
  >   *(i) that you cannot settle the complaint;*
  >
  >   *(ii) of the name and website address of an alternative dispute resolution (ADR) approved body which would be competent to deal with the complaint; and*
  >
  >   *(iii) whether you agree to use the scheme operated by that body.*

8.5: You ensure that complaints are dealt with promptly, fairly, and free of charge.

- The firm must be confident that the complaints process is appropriate.
- The firm must be confident that it will have the evidence to counter any assertion that a complaint has not been handled correctly. In practice, this often means that it is sensible for the firm to designate an individual as the person responsible for complaints. That person ought to have the necessary resources and skills to ensure that a timely, reputable and consistent way of dealing with issues can be developed.
- Complaints should be reviewed for lessons learned. Do complaints have a common theme (for example, do clients regularly complain about lack of communication by fee earners)? Does a particular department have a disproportionate number of complaints? Is one individual receiving too many complaints and does this suggest a training or other need? Does complaint handling garner intelligence that should be shared with the compliance officers?

What lessons can we learn from the Ombudsman?

Consider this statement made by the Ombudsman in a 2014 report about conveyancing services,[64] but containing a client perspective that is equally relevant to other work streams:

At the end of the day, people just want their house purchase or sale to go through with the minimum of fuss – a reasonable expectation when you're a paying customer. 'Fixed fee' and 'no move, no fee' agreements are fundamentally great innovations in a legal industry that has been hit hard by economic austerity. It is an increasingly consumer led market in which people want to know where they stand and then budget accordingly. I anticipate it will be those lawyers and non-lawyers behind many of these innovations who can also commit to greater levels of customer care that ultimately prosper. This means keeping to agreements over cost, ensuring delays are kept to a minimum, and maintaining good lines of communication. If lawyers stick to these simple principles I predict they won't go far wrong.

We have already mentioned the collaborative work of the Ombudsman and the SRA. A recently published joint research document gives us some insights into why LeO may need to become involved in complaint investigation with many lessons that can be taken from the findings and fed into internal management strategies.

The report is titled "Research into the experiences and effectiveness of solicitors' first tier complaints handling processes" and it provides information about client expectations and the cause of failures.[65]

Very broadly, some of the headline findings focused on the following:
- Users of legal services want regular communication about progress, clear information about costs and information about the legal process. When questioned, only 23% of law firms thought that consumers' key expectations included a clear explanation about the legal process.
- Whilst most law firms say that they comply with the requirement to provide information about their complaints procedure at the start of the matter, 37% of service users said they were not told about the procedure. This may indicate that the way in which we present this regulatory information is not sufficiently transparent (for example, where it is included in client care or terms of business literature) or suited to the needs of the particular client.
- Not all firms comply with regulatory and legal duties at the end of the complaints process or signpost clients to the Ombudsman and/or alternative dispute agencies.
- Verbal expressions of dissatisfaction are complaints but many firms fail to recognise this.
- Some firms take too long to deal with a complaint.

Other interesting data is gleaned from the annual reports produced by LeO and available from the Ombudsman's website. For example, in

complaints data in respect of legal services providers (the majority of which are solicitors and SRA-authorised firms) released for 2018/19, the Ombudsman shows that there are some common causes for client complaint. The following categories are noteworthy:
- 25% – delay or failure to progress
- 21% – failure to advise
- 15% – failure to follow instructions
- 19% – costs
- 20% – poor communication

The research and data provides food for thought and clues as to what needs to happen in practice – simple things such as improving our communication skills with clients, keeping them advised, managing their expectations, telling them bad news about delays, and generally ensuring that there will be no surprises about the outcome of their matter or about the costs.

With this in mind, some concluding thoughts for managers and compliance officers to consider and incorporate into their strategies:
- In terms of our relationships with our clients, has the firm made its expectations clear about the behaviours it relies upon from everyone in the firm regardless of role, legal qualification or anything else?
- Do we have evidence that we clearly express what we can and will do for the client?
- Are we prepared to recognise that specific client needs may mean that we have to adapt standard methodologies in some circumstances?
- Is the financial aspect of the relationship clearly explained so that there will be no surprises about the level of our fees or any other payments that the client has to make?
- Do we listen to clients and respond to their concerns, questions etc in a timely and suitable manner?
- Do we all understand the very wide meaning of a complaint?

- Does everyone understand their personal role in handling complaints effectively?
- Do we continue to monitor the appropriateness of our client care and service delivery standards throughout the retainer?
- Do we review matters when completing the clients' instructions to ensure that we have met their expectations?

Key points from Section 2

Essential knowledge to manage compliance
- The relevant sections of the SRA Standards and Regulations – eg, the SRA Principles, SRA Codes – and Statement of Solicitor Competence plus any other sections that are a necessary part of your compliance strategy because of the work you do, people you employ etc.
- The terms of your authorised status.
- The relationship that all your employees have with the SRA – eg, does a solicitor have conditions upon their practising certificate or does a non-solicitor have a regulatory relationship with the SRA that prohibits or restricts your right to employ them?
- An identification of the risks to regulatory compliance that are present in your firm.
- Confidence that internal processes provide solutions.

Top tips to demonstrate regulatory compliance
- Ensure that there is senior management buy-in to regulatory compliance. Know that your partners are in agreement about the internal standards that they are willing to enforce.
- Ensure that the firm employs like-minded colleagues: test ethical responses at regular intervals.
- Develop a suite of policies that strengthen the firm's regulatory responses and facilitate a consistent response. There is safety with consistency. Implement effective monitoring processes to keep policies relevant and ensure people are complying.
- Do not assume everyone in the firm will know what behaviours you and the SRA expect of them; solicitors may misunderstand their duties or choose not to apply them and unqualified staff may be starting with a lower level of understanding. Respond to all this with training to deliver your messages.
- Training is the key to your compliance response: explain the

SRA's position and the firm's internal requirements and build on this knowledge to improve the ethical ambience.
- An important training message is that this is a complicated topic! Many regulatory and ethical matters require the use of judgement. The individual with a concern must not take a chance. A concern shared and discussed, and a firm-based response, places both the individual and the firm in a safer position.
- Identify the risks to ensuring that regulatory compliance standards are met and develop strategies to mitigate the situation. For example, less experienced litigators need to be mentored and supervised in an appropriate way to ensure that they have the confidence to challenge inappropriate pressures that may cast doubt over their duties towards the courts and the proper administration of justice.
- Ensure that internal communication channels are visible.
- Consider drawing on the regulatory requirements and including them in contracts of employment and partnership deeds. Use the competencies described in the Statement of Solicitor Competence and assess against them in appraisals and in connection with your performance-related pay programmes.
- Be very clear in delivering the message that mistakes will happen – no one is perfect. What happens next is important: it is far better to discuss mistakes in a timely and open fashion so that the firm's risk management strategies can be deployed.

Regulatory compliance in practice – the golden rules

- Having a relationship with the SRA is not open for debate. In order for a solicitor to remain licensed to practice, and a law firm to continue to be authorised, there must be an understanding that the SRA has a statutory duty to oversee both individual and entity.
- Regulatory compliance requires an understanding of SRA

Key points from Section 2

expectations. These are set out in the SRA Standards and Regulations.
- Regulatory expectations have their origins in legal and ethical duties.
- Ethics is the foundation stone upon which we build client relationships. Ethics is good for business; the majority of clients want to receive an ethical service.
- Ethical behaviour must never be cast aside, even in circumstances where it could be argued that a particular action was linked with a need to act in a client's best interests or was a result of client or other pressure.
- Effective law firm management will enable an employee to act ethically.
- Proper governance and risk management means that systems and processes are developed to enable an ethical environment for employees to provide services.
- A key message is that openness and accountability outweigh any inclination not to be transparent about poor judgement calls, complaints etc.
- Regulatory compliance expectations are that the firm will have a transparent relationship with all regulators and ombudsmen. This means that an understanding of the role of the Legal Ombudsmen is essential, as is an acknowledgement of any further regulatory bodies that may have a right to have an interest in the firm (for example, those law firms that are also authorised to provide financial services will need to consider the Financial Conduct Authority and the Financial Ombudsman Service).
- Documented evidence of compliance is essential if you are to have a fuss-free relationship with your regulator. Do you have the audit trail to prove your statements are true?

Section 3:
Compliance with legal obligations

Introduction

In a book with the title *Regulation, Compliance and Ethics* it would be understandable if we forgot to consider the duty to act legally. Yet of course we must.

The SRA Standards and Regulations leave us in no doubt about the expectations:

- SRA Principle 1: You act in a way that upholds the constitutional principle of the rule of law and the proper administration of justice.
- SRA Codes of Conduct: you keep up to date with and follow the law and regulation governing the way you work.

There is therefore a direct correlation between legal compliance and regulatory interest in us. SRA enforcement action demonstrates the consequences of a breach of these regulatory duties.

Case study

Consider the matter of Stephen Pickard. Mr Pickard was a solicitor who was sentenced to eight years in prison in 2016 for his involvement in a fraudulent investment scheme. His conduct was referred to the SDT[66] on the basis that his involvement suggested that he had breached SRA Principles in respect of the duty to uphold the rule of law and to act with integrity; as well as duties of trust and confidence. The SDT ordered that Mr Pickard be struck off the roll of solicitors. The findings included the following commentary:

> His actions were planned and were in direct breach of his position as a trusted solicitor.
>
> His misconduct had been hugely impactful on those members of the public that had been the victims of the fraudulent schemes. Further, the matter had been reported locally, nationally and internationally. Headlines such as "Another lawyer helps fraudsters by giving credibility to their scam" undoubtedly harmed the reputation of the profession.
>
> The Respondent knew that his actions were in material breach of his obligation to protect the public and the reputation of the profession.
>
> He had lent his name to fraudulent schemes to give them credence.

Not only do incidents of this nature have potentially severe consequences for the individual concerned, there are implications for the firms in which they are employed. Any wrongdoing can also cause commercial and reputational damage. Additionally, many of the laws to which we are subject derive from other regulatory sources, extending the scrutiny over us and what we are doing.

More than that, what individuals do outside office hours may well have an impact on the ability to continue to work within the industry and/or their disciplinary records. A spate of recent disciplinary investigations have involved private use of social media and similar non-work-related activities.[67]

For all these reasons, compliance with the professional standards connected with effective governance in chapter 2 of the SRA Code of Conduct for Firms must incorporate strategies to manage the risk of legal breach events occurring.

In this section, we look primarily at the legislation that must be considered within the workplace, first making a checklist of the legislation and either including it or discounting it from the compliance programme.

We then look in more detail at two particularly high-risk and legally based compliance priorities that arise in practice in respect of anti-money laundering and data protection obligations, and include basic knowledge with compliance strategies and input from thought leaders.

The focus on compliance duties connected with anti-money laundering and data protection legislation, with suggestions about how to demonstrate compliance in practice, is deliberate. These are two topics that are included in the SRA Risk Outlook. There is scrutiny over our collective response not only by the SRA but also by other regulatory bodies and even by government. It is hard to imagine that there are many firms for whom these laws will not be a consideration, and breach will almost certainly result not only in legal action but also regulatory censure and adverse publicity for the firm. Whilst the knowledge it is necessary to acquire is different with respect to each subject, the compliance strategies can be considered in a wider context and as a response in all compliance contexts.

Chapter 9:
An overview of legal compliance

Introduction

For the reasons described in the introduction to this section, law firm management and compliance responses must include identification of all the laws that are relevant.

Whilst it is not the purpose of this book to give legal guidance, the following is intended to provide assistance with a broad explanation of the scope of this topic.

There are three distinct legislative categories to consider:

Practice-related laws

These are laws that are relevant because we are solicitors or employed in SRA-authorised law firms, or because of the type of firm in which we practise.

Consider the table below and the compliance checklist – a useful starting point.

Understanding and demonstrating compliance with these sources of legal duty sits sensibly with the senior management team, the COLP and the practice manager. Failure to comply would require notification to the SRA in accordance with regulatory notification duties.

In addition, there are a number of legislative duties arising in respect

Section 3: Compliance with legal obligations

Table 13: Legal compliance checklist

Legislation	Compliance checklist
Solicitors Act 1974	Legislation relating to rights to practise as a solicitor with various provisions relating to admission, practising certificates, the position of unqualified persons, disciplinary powers etc. Once admitted to the roll of solicitors, an individual must hold a current practising certificate if he or she is employed in private practice in connection with the provision of legal services. Questions for you: Are we confident that all our solicitors are entitled to, and hold, a practising certificate? What measures do we take to ensure that we notify the SRA about any concerns we might have about individual solicitors? Are we confident that we do not hold out, explicitly or implicitly, non-solicitors in such a way that they may be misrepresenting their status?
Administration of Justice Act 1985	Further legislation describing statutory requirements arising in connection with the administration of justice.
Courts and Legal Services Act 1990	As above, including updating provisions relating to the oversight of solicitors.
Legal Services Act 2007	The legislation that sets out the regulatory objectives and professional principles; creates the Legal Services Board; defines the meaning of reserved legal activities and offences that arise in respect of the unlawful delivery of reserved activity services; defines approved regulator roles; makes alternative business structures (ABS) lawful; creates the current legal complaints process; and includes many miscellaneous provisions about lawyers. Questions for you: Are we confident that we lawfully manage the position with regard to the conduct of reserved legal activities? Do we only outsource non-reserved legal activities? If we are an ABS, are we aware of, and do we comply with, the various statutory restrictions on how we practise?

continued on next page

Legislation	Compliance checklist
Companies Act/Limited Liability Partnership Act	SRA-authorised firms are entitled to be limited companies or limited liability partnerships. These are, of course, statutorily defined entities. **Questions for you:** Do we comply with all statutory duties that arise because of our corporate status?

of the firm's role as an employer. It is essential that the various employer-related statutes are understood and applied correctly because breach may have an impact on the regulatory relationship. Similarly, in terms of the firm's marketing and promotional work, not only must this be in compliance with the SRA Standards and Regulations requirements (notably the publicity and confidentiality considerations in the SRA Codes of Conduct), but it must also satisfy legislative standards such as those overseen by the Advertising Standards Agency and the data considerations (such as how publicity is communicated to the recipient) overseen by the Information Commissioner's Office.

Laws applied on behalf of clients

Only you will know what these are from a consideration of your various work streams.

In order to comply with SRA Principles, the SRA Codes and the Statement of Solicitor Competence, all solicitors must be satisfied that in respect of the legislation applied on behalf of clients, they

- provide a proper standard of service to their clients;
- ensure that managers and employees are competent to carry out their role, and to keep their professional knowledge and skills, as well as their understanding of their legal, ethical and regulatory obligations, up to date; and
- maintain an adequate and up-to-date understanding of relevant law, policy and practice (A2d, Statement of Solicitor Competence).

And this is equally relevant to non-solicitors, regardless of any legal qualification they may or may not hold. As we have seen, the SRA Principles and SRA Code of Conduct for Firms apply to them not because of their status but because of their employment in an SRA-authorised firm. Also, despite the fact that the Statement of Competence does not have any direct application, the content is in any event best practice. Knowledge of current and relevant law is essential to comply with the SRA Standards and Regulations and avoid the risks attached to giving wrong or negligent advice.

Within this second category, it is also necessary to consider the laws that are relevant because of the nature of the work and that place restrictions on the service provider. For example, personal injury solicitors and their colleagues must ensure that they understand and can work within the legal restrictions in the Legal Aid, Sentencing and Punishment of Offenders Act 2012 and the Section 56 prohibition on making or accepting payments for the referral of clients in personal injury matters.

When considering compliance in practice, does the management strategy extend to identifying relevant technical knowledge and committing training solutions to ensure that individuals are competent and thereby able to provide a proper standard of service? This will be a senior management lead but responsibility to oversee application can be delegated to department heads, team leaders and supervisors. Monitoring can be achieved through file review, supervisory intelligence and using complaints data.

Other laws

In addition to laws that apply to the profession and those that must be used for the benefit of clients, there are a number of regulatory laws, and laws designed to protect individuals and their rights, that we must understand and observe.

These laws apply to us because we run businesses and we are service providers. The table below provides a non-exhaustive list that you will want to consider.

Chapter 9: An overview of legal compliance

Table 14: Other legislation

Legislation	Some duties imposed on law firms	Compliance checklist
Bribery Act 2010	It is a criminal offence to make or accept bribes. The law includes a corporate offence for failure on the part of an entity (which includes SRA-authorised law firms) to prevent an offence being committed by its employees with a defence by means of policies designed to prevent this.	Do we explain to our colleagues what payments can lawfully be made or accepted? Do we have a formal anti-bribery and corruption policy? Do we communicate our expectations about gifts and hospitality? Do we have records to substantiate our stated requirements?
Equality Act 2010	This Act consolidates previous equality laws and protects nine protected characteristics from direct and indirect discrimination, harassment and victimisation. This applies to law firms as service providers and as employers. The offences can result in criminal charges. There is a nexus between this legislation, the regulatory objectives in the Legal Services Act 2007 (for example, in respect to access to justice and the creation of an independent, diverse, strong and effective profession) and the STaRs. Any solicitor or law firm convicted of an offence under the Equality Act is likely to also be disciplined by the SRA.	Can we demonstrate that in our employment policies and our treatment of clients and all third parties, we have complied with equality legislation? Do we communicate our expectations about behaviours to our workforce and third-party suppliers, deliver training as necessary, and monitor their compliance? Do we have systems for handling complaints based on equality issues? Have we considered the way in which we adapt service provision to comply with legislation? Do we keep up to date with case law developments?
Financial Services and Markets Act 2000	This is an often forgotten piece of legislation. It applies to the provision of financial services in the UK and creates the regulatory framework for the financial services industry. It is a criminal offence for an unregulated person to provide financial services unless they can	Have we identified whether we perform regulated activities and whether we need to be authorised by the Financial Conduct Authority? If we are exempt, are we able to demonstrate to the regulator that we comply

continued on next page

Section 3: Compliance with legal obligations

Legislation	Some duties imposed on law firms	Compliance checklist
	rely on exemptions and exclusions in the legislation. Solicitors can rely on these to provide certain financial services to their clients. However, this is in very narrowly defined circumstances; to carry on exempt regulated activities they must comply with financial services rules made by the SRA (and approved by the Financial Conduct Authority) or to carry on excluded activities the firm must be satisfied that they can fulfil all attached conditions. There are many pitfalls.	with the SRA Handbook requirements that apply to financial services (ie, the SRA Financial Services (Scope) Rules 2001 and the SRA Financial Services (Conduct of Business) Rules 2001). Do we need to deliver training? Are we keeping accurate records?
Proceeds of Crime Act 2002	This is the primary anti-money laundering legislation in the UK and creates offences (and defences) relating to this activity.	Are we managing the risk that we may facilitate money laundering offences?
Terrorism Act 2000	This is similar to the Proceeds of Crime Act, but has application in the area of the prevention of funding of terrorist organisations.	As above, but in respect of terrorist funding.
Money Laundering Regulations 2019	This applies to certain firms providing relevant services in the regulated sector. Its purpose is to provide audit trails, information gathering, record-keeping and disclosure duties. Failures may result in the commission of offences.	Does this legislation apply to us? Do we have the audit trail to satisfy record-keeping, risk assessment requirements and similar?
Criminal Finances Act 2017	This is a newer piece of legislation which took effect in autumn 2017. It has many provisions that strengthen the anti-money laundering toolkit for law enforcement agencies, introduces tax evasion offences and includes an offence of facilitating tax evasion on the part of another	Given that this is a new piece of legislation, have we identified the risks of committing an offence? Do we need to roll out training? Have we an internal policy to deal with the issues?

continued on next page

Legislation	Some duties imposed on law firms	Compliance checklist
	person in the UK or elsewhere. There is a corporate offence where a firm will be labile for the actions of its employees and a defence that suitable measures to prevent this have been introduced.	
Data Protection Act 2018 & General Data Protection Regulation	Data protection legislation is designed to regulate the processing of personal data belonging to data subjects by data controllers and data processors. This requires controllers/processors to comply with data protection principles and gives data subjects rights in respect of the processing. This legislation is enforced by the Information Commissioner's Office (ICO) in the UK. The ICO has numerous powers under the legislation including the power to fine defaulting controllers/processors and to take other enforcement action.	Have we evidence to demonstrate our accountability to the ICO? Do we have processes to deal with data subject rights? What training, monitoring etc needs to be added to our existing internal processes?

Chapter 10:
Managing the money laundering risk

It is not the purpose of this book to provide the reader with a detailed explanation of money laundering. Whilst we will provide an overview of the topic and the relevant law, and flag up overlapping related legal duties arising in respect of terrorist funding, sanctions, tax evasion issues and similar, this is not intended to be a substitute for your own study of these topics.

Rather, we will focus on why compliance with this legal requirement is essential, with strategies to demonstrate compliance in practice, and a consideration of the consequences of getting the firm's response wrong.

The bigger picture – what the UK wants to achieve

Money laundering is not good for the UK. Bad money often inflates property prices. Fraud deprives the economy of finances. Corruption enables terrorism to be funded. Estimates are just estimates (no one completes a declaration to confirm the amount of money or other criminal property they hide) but it is said that in excess of £90 billion may be laundered in the UK each year. The UK wants to reverse this picture. The government wants to make the UK an uninviting and hostile place in which to launder criminal property. For this to happen, we are all expected to play a defensive role and professionals are tasked with a role in the enforcement of the legislation.

"It is said that in excess of £90 billion may be laundered in the UK each year. The UK wants to reverse this picture."

Why lawyers must prioritise this risk

The SRA says:

Legal professionals should be aware that they are vulnerable to being targeted by criminals because of the skills, services and products they provide which can facilitate money laundering, and the legitimacy they can lend to a criminal's activities.[68]

As the comment above illustrates, managing and mitigating the risks associated with money laundering and associated crime is a government priority. The government and other external stakeholders identify the legal profession as one of the main facilitators in the money laundering process and identify the need for vigilance and understanding of how we will be targeted.

Such involvement, accidental or otherwise, is also one of the risk priorities identified by the SRA in the Risk Outlook 2019/20.[69] The SRA explains its reasoning and expectations as follows:

If you or your firm facilitates money laundering, then you are helping to fund serious and organised crime. By preventing money laundering, you and your firm play a major role in reducing the threat to the UK, its citizens and its institutions.

This is not a new thought. Money laundering risk has featured in all Risk Outlooks since 2014. Reasons for this include the following:

- Other bodies have an interest in our role as a deterrent and they are vocal in their views on our perceived shortcomings.

    Recent governments have done much to strengthen the UK's deterrence systems and have undertaken studies into the topic. For example, two National Risk Assessments have been published since 2015; both are critical of the role that legal professionals play. In 2015, for example, the money laundering risk within the industry was assessed to be high. This focused on the following issues:
    - complicit lawyers who facilitate money laundering by enabling criminals to access legal services and the regulated sector;

- risks associated with negligent or unwitting legal professionals who facilitate conveyancing through misunderstandings or ignorance, particularly through the use of property transactions and access to the firm's client account; and
- the existence of negligent legal professionals who do not comply with their obligations under the Proceeds of Crime Act 2002, such that client due diligence and suspicious activity reporting is undermined.

The criticism does not stop there. Additionally, there has been commentary about the response of the profession to the topic from the National Crime Agency (NCA). You will be aware that we must report our knowledge and suspicions to the NCA. This is the suspicious activity report (SAR) regime.

The NCA publishes annual statistics revealing the number of reports it receives from each part of the regulated sector. In the 2017 Report,[70] for example, we were told that for the period from October 2015 to March 2017, the NCA received 634,113 SARs, of which only 4,878 (0.77%) were submitted by independent legal professionals. This is an undeniably low figure. The report authors do not give a view on this volume, saying that "it is for the sectors and their supervisors to assess if the volume of SARs submitted is proportionate to the risks their sectors face". There has been less restraint in previous reports – in 2014 the fact that the numbers of reports that were submitted by lawyers had decreased was queried.

In addition, there has been criticism of the quality of reporting from the legal sector, such that in 2014 the NCA announced that it would not accept any consent SARs that were incomplete.

None of this commentary can be ignored by the SRA. As an approved regulator, and a risk-based regulator at that, it has a function to monitor confidence in the profession. Indeed, it now has a role as a professional body AML supervisor under the Money Laundering Regulations and is overseen in this supervisory body by a regulator known as the Office for Professional Body AML Supervision (OPBAS). This extends beyond client confidence to the need to monitor the confidence that interested stakeholders must have in us.

- Much of the legislation is aimed as much at us as it is the criminals.

Whilst we must understand the principal money laundering offences indicated in the Proceeds of Crime Act and, of course, avoid the commission of these offences, it is more likely that we will commit secondary offences that are included, such as failing to report our knowledge or suspicions and/or inadvertently or otherwise tipping off an individual in a way that prejudices anti-money laundering legislation. Solicitors and others working in SRA-authorised firms have been convicted of such offences with the consequences extending to prison sentences and the right to practise law and remain employed in law firms removed.

Cases that have been reported include *R v Griffiths & Pattison*,[71] in which Mr Griffiths, a solicitor, was convicted of a failure to report an offence under the Proceeds of Crime Act 2002 and served a prison sentence.

Other legislation, too, contains offences that are aimed as much at us as at criminals.

For example, the Serious Organised Crime Act 2015 was designed to strengthen the UK's response to organised crime. It includes an offence so that those who enable – including professional enablers such as solicitors and others – the criminal activities of an organised crime group can be prosecuted: a person who participates in the criminal activities of an organised crime group commits an offence. It is clear that a person will be guilty if he or she knows or reasonably suspects that their contribution, or participation, will, *inter alia*, help an organised crime group to perform criminal activities.

The significance of this offence must not be underestimated.

An organised crime group is defined as a group of three or more individuals which has as its purpose, or one of its purposes, the carrying on of criminal activities. The legal reach is wide; a solicitor or other legal professional may be guilty of committing an offence even without knowing the identity of the crime group – they may not be his or her clients but the individuals on the other side of a matter.

A further development with similar trends is the Criminal Finances Act 2017. This Act notably includes tax evasion offences with a direct bearing on us. Companies etc will be held criminally liable for failing to prevent the criminal facilitation of a tax evasion offence by an employee or an external agent, even in circumstances where the employer was not involved in the act or aware of it. A defence is available if the employer can demonstrate that it has implemented reasonable preventative measures such as the inclusion of an anti-tax evasion policy in its internal systems and processes.

- We undertake many high-risk activities that are useful to criminals.

  Many of the legal services we provide are useful to criminals wishing to launder funds. Conveyancing is the obvious work stream and, indeed, we are advised by the SRA that one-third of all anti-money laundering reports over the three-year period to 2017 related to residential conveyancing – three times more than with any other type of legal service.

  Notwithstanding this statistic, we ignore the risks attached to other work streams at our peril. There are specific risks attached to other areas of work, for example:
  - private client work – criminal property in estate administration work;
  - trust work – the use of trusts as money laundering vehicles;
  - charity work – use of a charity to launder funds or as a vehicle for terrorist finding activities;

- attorney/deputyship instructions – misuse of the power resulting in acquisition, use or similar of criminal property;
- company/commercial work – company formations for fraudulent purposes, creation of complex corporate transactions to house criminal property, complicated private equity and collective investment schemes;
- litigation – sham litigation to facilitate money laundering; and
- family work – use of criminal property, providing banking facilities.

We also maintain client accounts which, if misused by criminals, can be used to launder money. This risk is exacerbated in circumstances where we not only launder funds but also provide banking facilities to clients. In regulatory compliance terms, we must not provide banking facilities as this places us in breach of Rule 3.3 of the SRA Accounts Rules 2019:

You must not use a client account to provide banking facilities to clients or third parties. Payments into, and transfers or withdrawals from a client account must be in respect of the delivery by you of regulated services.

The SRA considers this to be a high risk to its regulatory objectives. Case law has developed the response to the issue and the SRA has referred a number of solicitors to the SDT for banking issues.

Case study

Consider the court case[72] and SDT investigation in respect of Fuglers LLP and three of the partners of that firm. The circumstances were that Fuglers acted for a football club. The club's bank account was withdrawn after a winding-up petition was brought by HM Revenue & Customs (HMRC). The club was insolvent. Over a period of four months, approximately £10 million of the club's money passed through Fuglers' client account. The SDT fined Fuglers £50,000 and its two managers £5,000 and £20,000. They appealed against the amount of the fines. The High Court dismissed the appeal and confirmed the seriousness of the misconduct that had been found by the SDT.

In the High Court judgment, reasons were given as to why client accounts should not be used as banking facilities:
- it was objectionable in itself;
- there was the risk of money laundering; and
- it impacted on insolvency processes.

Interest in this topic is not waning.

There are many reasons why legal initiatives, and regulatory interest, will not lessen in the short to medium term.

We are all too aware of terrorist attacks, which are of course funded through either the proceeds of crime or with clean money that has been successfully donated unnoticed to terrorist operations.

We also know that professionals – solicitors and accountants – have been publicly named and shamed in connection with the Panama Papers and Paradise Papers incidents. Solicitors have experienced the reputational fallout of being associated with these matters and criticised for alleged disregard of duties of confidentiality.

We are aware that the government has a motivation to dissuade criminals from seeking to use criminal property in the United Kingdom and that it is strengthening its toolkit. For example, we are told that in excess of £180 million worth of UK property has been the subject of criminal enquiry as the suspected proceeds of crime since 2004. Dirty money distorts property prices. Recent additions to legislative powers include undisclosed wealth orders and more transparency measures.

We know that the UK is being observed from further afield. The Financial Action Task Force, an international organisation with the remit to develop anti-money laundering and counter-terrorist finance initiatives, undertook an evaluation of the UK's anti-money laundering regime in 2018.

> "There are many reasons why legal initiatives, and regulatory interest, will not lessen in the short to medium term."

The basic knowledge

This is largely knowledge of the law, and we are expected to have availed ourselves of it. We must understand the following legislation and incorporate strategies into our internal processes to demonstrate an appropriate response to the risk of non-compliance and committing offences:
- The Proceeds of Crime Act 2002
- The Terrorism Act 2000
- The Money Laundering and Terrorist Financing (Amendment) Regulations 2019
- Criminal Finances Act 2017

Strategies to demonstrate compliance

Be under no illusions, the SRA expects no less than clear evidence that we have considered the risks of being targeted by criminals and can demonstrate a tailored and proportionate response to the identified risks.

The following checklist and table provide guidance about the questions that should be considered when tailoring an appropriate compliance response to deliver the correct assurances to the regulator:

- What services do we offer?

    The Proceeds of Crime Act and Terrorism Act apply regardless of type of work.

    Other ancillary legislation may also be relevant, depending on the services you provide. For example, the Money Laundering Regulations (MLR) will apply in circumstances where you are an 'independent legal professional' (ie, a law firm or a sole practitioner who by way of business provides legal or notarial services to other persons) undertaking 'relevant' business in the regulated sector.

    Relevant business encompasses the following activities:
    - buying and selling of real property or business entities;
    - managing of client money, securities or other assets;

- opening or management of bank, savings or securities accounts;
- organisation of contributions necessary for the creation, operation or management of companies; and
- creation, operation or management of trusts, companies, foundations or similar structures.

- If we are subject to the MLR, have we considered the steps that must be taken to demonstrate compliance?

The table below will help with the detail of your response.

Table 15: MLR compliance checklist

Step	Action
Step 1	Undertake the mandatory firm-wide risk assessment that is required to comply with Regulation 18. A written risk assessment must be produced. This can build on your existing risk reflections and registers etc, which will be improved using the pointers in the MLR (ie, think about your clients, country/geographic factors, services, delivery means etc) and the guidance issued by the SRA, plus the Legal Sector Affinity Group Anti-Money Laundering Guidance for the Legal Sector. Much of the SRA's recent supervisory work in this area has been to consider whether there is compliance with this obligation. **Questions for you:** What are the risks attributable to our work streams? Do our people create any risks to compliance? What risks are attributable to any geographical considerations? How will we ensure that we communicate our risk analysis to colleagues and monitor that this is understood? How will we ensure that the risk assumptions are accurate? How often will we review the risk assessment?
Step 2	Reflect on the firm's existing internal controls and review and reformat these to suit the firm's assessment of the risks that it attracts and to accommodate the MLR. **Questions for you:** How do we ensure that we have an individual risk assessment for each file? Who will be responsible for individual risk assessments? What processes do we need to make sure that the money laundering reporting officer and other senior members of the firm are made aware of high-risk scenarios? What other policies will support our risk response? Do we need to roll out

continued on next page

Section 3: Compliance with legal obligations

Step	Action
	guidance to deal with common questions? How will we ensure that there is ongoing monitoring of risk throughout a retainer? How will we monitor for continuing suitability of the policies and compliance by our colleagues?
Step 3	Consider subsidiaries and branches where the firm is a parent undertaking and developing ways in which similar risk measures can be rolled out.
Step 4	Appoint a board member (the money laundering reporting officer, partner or similar) to take responsibility at senior level and appoint an individual tasked with the independent audit function. Question for you: Is this a good opportunity/excuse to include more members of the firm in a compliance function and to strengthen the governance and reporting lines (which will serve the additional purpose of providing the SRA with evidence of demonstrating an appropriate response to effective governance standards as required in chapter 2 of the SRA Code of Conduct for Firms)?
Step 5	Introduce processes for the screening of relevant employees for AML risk awareness, conduct and integrity values. Bear in mind that the Regulations impose this obligation on you before making any new appointments and also whilst the individual is employed in the business. The latter can be tied in with training. Questions for you: What will you do to ensure that the employment process includes this screening? How will you ensure that training identifies any people-related risks?
Step 6	Training must include the data protection topic so far as this relates to the safe retention and destruction of personal data collected for MLR purposes. Questions for you: Is this the time to take a fresh approach to training solutions? Can this be tied in with the need for solicitors to demonstrate they have appropriate skills and behaviours as required by the Solicitors Competence Statement?
Step 7	Reflect on internal client due diligence processes. We are being expected to use more sophisticated risk analysis techniques and to extend our diligence measures in respect of companies and certain trusts and to all (foreign and domestic) Politically Exposed Persons. Questions for you: Who has responsibility for this task? Are your people equipped to do this?

continued on next page

Step	Action
	Are you confident that fee earners are taking responsibility for this process and not delegating their responsibilities to support staff and thereby increasing the risks of non-compliance? Is it clear that any concerns or queries should be raised in a timely way?
Step 8	Reliance measures need to be documented and staff trained in what is suitable. **Questions for you:** Again, is it time to revisit the firm's policy on when reliance is an acceptable means of fulfilling obligations? What safety messages should you communicate to colleagues?
Step 9	Personal data must be processed for MLR identification purposes only and must be destroyed after five years unless the client gives consent for its retention or there is a legal reason why the information must be retained. **Questions for you:** Most law firms retain documentation for longer than five years. Do you have proper authority to do this? Does your client care literature/privacy notice need to be reviewed?

- Do we have a system for the internal reporting of knowledge and suspicions?
- What audit trail do we need to roll out to ensure that we have the evidence that suspicions etc are being reported?
- What resources does the MLRO need to fulfil their statutory duty?
- How will we ensure that our response remains in line with latest requirements?
- What will be our risk management response in circumstances where we are not under a legal duty to comply with the MLR?

AN INSIDER'S INSIGHT

Emma Oettinger was the financial crime policy adviser for the Law Society of England and Wales for six years, and spent three years at HM Treasury leading teams undertaking domestic anti-money laundering policy and financial sanctions implementation. She co-chaired the FATF typology on the vulnerability of legal professionals to money laundering and terrorist financing and now provides advice on a range of financial crime issues at Ashurst, a leading global law firm. In the following contribution, she provides her thoughts on how to ensure the appropriate response to the need to demonstrate compliance in this area.

Turning compliance into business opportunity
While compliance by law firms with AML obligations may be driven by legal or professional conduct requirements, I have found over the years that the fear of penalties is not actually a great motivator for compliance. This is especially where there is perceived to be a very small likelihood of being involved in money laundering and even less likelihood of penalties being applied.

There are three key areas to focus on to boost engagement within the firm.

Senior management buy-in
If senior management are not seen to comply with AML obligations, it will be very difficult to get anyone else to. While legal obligations should catch the attention of your senior management team, wider commercial considerations are likely to resonate more.

The commercial considerations include client expectations and profit.

The days of simply sending your own engagement terms to clients and insisting they sign them are on the wane, with many large clients now sending their own engagement terms (especially for panel *engagements) to be signed by the law firms. These terms are increasingly requiring firms to meet standards on AML, sanctions, bribery, modern slavery and other supply chain risk mitigation, irrespective of the scope of legal requirements in place in a jurisdiction. Failure to meet those expectations for all client intake puts those client relationships and possible panel membership at risk.*

Further, many firms are developing advisory capacity for clients in relation to a range of compliance areas. Investigations into or findings against the firm for its own failings in these areas will have a significant negative consequence for the revenue in that practice area. The revenue lost from these opportunities can quickly outweigh the internal costs of compliance.

Align finance, risk and intake

Your finance team and whoever is responsible for risk assessment and client intake need to be pulling in the same direction. Money laundering warning signs do not just occur at inception, but quite often will occur in the time-pressured lead-up to closure of a deal.

Make sure your finance team understand the warning signs and when to escalate. It will enable you to have a united front when inevitably you get unexpected money on account, requests to bill someone other the client or to send money held on account somewhere other than expected. This helps manage money laundering risk as well as meet professional requirements around the client account and prevent attempts at tax evasion.

Communicate in a clear and relevant manner

An off-the-shelf online training programme for the whole firm may seem a cost-effective way of ticking the AML training box. However, particularly after the first time of taking it, the impact on behaviour in the firm is likely to quickly diminish.

To really drive engagement, you need to design your training with your audience in mind.

- *If you have a centralised team doing client intake, they will need more information about the details of how to do client due diligence. Your partners and fee earners will only need that information at a very high level and it is better to focus them on warning signs and what you want them to do when they have concerns.*
- *Equally, stories about local drug dealers and grannies with biscuit tins full on money under the bed are not going to engage a group of corporate partners who work with multi-nationals on M&A deals or structured financing; while the Rolls Royce and BAE cases won't mean that much to your local conveyancer or probate practitioner.*

Training makes sense when it is put in context
- *Most lawyers are of the view that they don't have criminals as clients, and actually the vast majority of clients and matters will not involve money laundering.*
- *However, as a firm you are operating within a given economy and you will not be immune to the financial crime and other criminal activity that is occurring within that economy. Use national risk assessments, financial intelligence unit annual reports, publications from professional bodies and civil society and press reports to help explain what crime is currently happening in your area or the economy in which you operate.*

Training has an impact when it is practical
- *Most lawyers don't think like criminals – but they love stories – so examples, particularly relevant examples, will be far more engaging than simply teaching the legal or professional requirements.*
- *One of the big challenges in providing training examples is that real life cases are often reported in brief, with the benefit of hindsight, and come across as very obvious criminality that no*

self-respecting lawyer would get involved in. In reality, financial crime very rarely looks like financial crime when it walks in the door.
- *As money laundering offences are often drawn quite widely, including a range of regulatory offences, it is quite easy for clients, especially business clients, to find themselves on the wrong side of money laundering law without really meaning to.*
- *So build your examples around a client and matter that fits the normal profile for your firm. Start out with everything looking normal and unremarkable. Then slowly add in warning signs from a range of areas including conflicts, ethics, commercial and financial crime. Take the audience through the process of considering this client and matter, adding new information and asking them their thoughts as you go along. The IBA best practice guide[73] also has lots of information on warning signs and methodologies.*

By getting your legal teams to see the importance of understanding their client and the matters they are working on through a financial crime lens, they can start asking more incisive questions of the client, get more complete instructions, and be able to offer solutions to problems that the clients were not themselves aware they were facing.

And that is when your training has turned AML from a compliance programme to a new business opportunity.

Sanctions – a point about a common misunderstanding

The need to have an anti-money laundering process is on the radar of most law firms' compliance antennae. The risks do not relate to lack of a compliance response, but rather to an inappropriate response that is devoid of meaningful commitment to the cause internally.

At least there is a starting point from which to improve. This is not always the same in respect of the final topic in this chapter: sanctions. It is not uncommon for otherwise well-managed law firms not to have considered the application of sanctions in connection with the services that are delivered.

Sanctions are the penalties or restrictions imposed by international, regional or national authorities which are used to try to change the behaviours of a particular country or regime or to restrict the funding of individuals, entities or groups associated with terrorist or other criminal activity. There are many types of sanctions; economic, trade, financial or travel sanctions are commonplace.

We must ensure that we have appropriate processes to ensure that sanction restrictions are not circumvented. Whilst it may still be possible to provide services to a sanctioned client, this is usually subject to the grant of a licence or similar from the Treasury. Failure to comply may result in criminal prosecution for the firm concerned.

AN INSIDER'S INSIGHT

We have already had **Emma Oettinger**'s analysis of the benefits of a positive anti-money laundering response. Here is her message about sanctions:

Law firms, especially those who operate predominantly in a domestic context, can often take the view that sanctions happen to other people in foreign places, but there are at least three areas where sanctions can be relevant even to domestic law firms:

- *Sanctions can be imposed on individuals and businesses based in your own jurisdiction. This is especially the case in relation to terrorism financers and returned terrorist fighters who may still need access to standard legal assistance (divorce, wills, property, employment etc).*
- *In a fast-moving political situation, sanctions can be imposed on existing international clients who have wide-ranging business interests. Even being listed on a major stock exchange is no guarantee that sanctions will not be applied.*

- *In a globalised economy, even local businesses can have business interests with sanctioned counter-parties or in jurisdictions where targeted sanctions apply. These could include financial institutions, exporters, importers, retailers, transport operators, tourism companies, construction firms and telecommunications operators, to name a few.*

To mitigate risk:
- *Understand what sanctions regimes are in place and the extent to which your client base and work areas overlap with those sanctions regimes.*
- *Know who you are advising, what you are doing for them and who your counter-parties are.*
- *Make sure your finance team understand your bank's payment policies around jurisdictions where sanctions apply.*
- *If you don't have a sanctions expert in your office, identify a sanctions expert in another firm who can be your go-to person in the event of a sanctions risk crystallising for a given client or matter.*

This is sound guidance and triggers the need to add the following questions to your compliance checklist:
- ✔ What is the likelihood that we will fall foul, inadvertently or otherwise, of sanctions controls?
- ✔ Do our policies need to be reviewed so that sanctions risk management is incorporated?
- ✔ What process can we use to check sanctions lists and how will we evidence this in our audit trail?
- ✔ Do we need to deliver training to our people?

Chapter 11: Managing the risks of handling data

Introduction

Data protection is another UK priority. This bigger picture must be understood by law firms and compliance strategies must respond to the legal duty to keep data safe. This is both a challenge because of the vast amount of data we process, but also something in respect of which we can claim an advantage over other businesses.

This is because we are starting in a different position to many of these other businesses and the underlying values that frame the legislation are familiar to us. We already have ethical and regulatory duties to keep clients' – and former and sometimes prospective clients' – information confidential. We are required to protect this source of information and (subject, of course, to certain legal overrides) keep clients' secrets secret. By and large, we are good at this and we know the consequences if we get it wrong. What the law requires us to do is extend this duty so that we protect the personal data of all data subjects in circumstances where we are processing their information.

Why this is an issue if we misjudge our response

As with our response to anti-money laundering duties, we are not a profession that can hide away and remain under the radar. As with anti-money laundering, there are external stakeholders who are able to hold us to account.

The ICO has statutory powers to monitor compliance with data protection and privacy legislation. This organisation has the right to enforce sanctions where breaches of these protections occur. The latest piece of legislation over which the ICO has assumed responsibility is the General Data Protection Regulation (GDPR) and the Data Protection Act 2018, which have applied since 25 May 2018. Organisations, including law firms that process the personal data of others, must comply with these requirements.

We already know that the ICO has expressed misgivings about legal services providers and the alleged lack of care that we have shown. In 2014, for example, the then incumbent Information Commissioner, Christopher Graham, published a warning in which he sounded the alarm on data breaches in the legal profession.

Mr Graham reported that the ICO had received reports of 15 data breaches in three months which had been caused by the acts or omissions of barristers and solicitors. Mr Graham commented as follows:[74]

> *The number of breaches reported by barristers and solicitors may not seem that high, but given the sensitive information they handle, and the fact that it is often held in paper files rather than secured by any sort of encryption, that number is troubling. It is important that we sound the alarm at an early stage to make sure this problem is addressed before a barrister or solicitor is left counting the financial and reputational damage of a serious data breach.*

The basic knowledge

As with anti-money laundering legislation, it is not the purpose of this book to be a law reference manual. Briefly, however, in terms of GDPR it is important to understand the following:

- that the purpose of GDPR is to protect the personal data of citizens;

- the meaning of these key terms:
  - personal data;
  - data processing;
  - data controller;
  - data processors;
  - data protection officer; and
  - data subjects.
- data protection principles; and
- the rights of data subjects.

Strategies to manage compliance with GDPR
Compliance with GDPR requires two steps:
- ensuring compliance; and
- maintaining compliance.

The first step requires a project plan, and the table below provides a checklist for this. The project needs to be manned by appropriate members of the firm so that all aspects of the legal duties are considered. For this reason, it would make sense to include within the project team colleagues such as partners and members of the management team, representatives from the human resources and IT departments and the compliance officers.

Section 3: Compliance with legal obligations

Ensuring compliance

Table 16: GDPR compliance plan checklist

Action point	Comments
Create personal/sensitive data database	This is your data mapping exercise and the foundation of an effective data response. All categories of data must be recorded, together with information about decisions as to the lawful grounds for processing; details of data processors with whom the data is shared; transfer details; the storage and destruction policies and similar. For example, we will process personal data to comply with the Money Laundering Regulations. This fact should be recorded, with details of the legal ground for processing (ie, to comply with legislation), how information is given to the data subject, details of where the data is stored, for how long (remembering that under MLR we are only entitled to retain data for these purposes for five years from the end of the relationship and any extension of this period must be in reliance of another legal ground) and information about destruction methods.
Review current storage arrangements	We are entitled to hold personal data for only as long as necessary and then destroy the same. Are we doing what we say? Do not forget that this duty includes both paper and electronic storage methods.
Review existing policies relating to data – terms of business/client care/data protection policy/privacy notice/storage/destruction	We must be transparent about data and the information we provide must be up to date. Do our policies etc reflect GDPR language and requirements?
Review current data protection communications with employees	Do not forget that firms hold extensive personal data about employees, former employees and even prospective employees. This personal data is protected by GDPR so the data protection principles apply and these colleagues are data subjects with entitlements. Is the information that is included

continued on next page

Action point	Comments
	in employment contracts, your office manual etc current? Does the HR team comply in respect of the personal data collected in connection with the interview process? Are appraisal records, disciplinary records etc processed correctly? Are we confident that we ask for strictly necessary information only? Do we have appropriate storage and destruction processes for these categories of data?
Update policies etc as necessary	Who will be responsible for the drafting/review exercises?
Compile list of data processors with whom personal data is shared	The firm is a data controller and will share personal data that it processes with data processors (third parties who have access to the personal data). The firm must be satisfied that it is transparent about this and also that it has documented evidence of the agreements with these third parties. Again, there must be awareness of all types of data sharing and this will apply both in respect of data relating to client matters and in respect of employee data.
Review/draft written agreements with data processors to comply with GDPR	Who will be responsible for the drafting/review exercises? Progress should be added to the data mapping exercise.
Compile list of data transfer activity outside EEA and review lists	GDPR is intended to protect the personal data of European citizens within the European Union. Care must be taken that if data is transferred outside the EU, the data controller has taken adequate steps to ensure similar protections and that the data subject is made aware of the location of their data. Again, this exercise is part of the data mapping exercise; any movement outside the EU must be recorded and steps must be taken to ensure that the data processor has adequate protections in place, and that the data subject is given accurate information.
Review marketing data – how obtained/for what purposes/ opt-in or opt-out	Marketing, particularly by email, is subject to protection in GDPR and other related legislation such as the Privacy and Electronic Communications Regulations. As part of the data marketing exercise, it is necessary to review all marketing activities, assess the legal ground relied upon to undertake marketing and, if the ground is the consent

continued on next page

Action point	Comments
	of the data subject, decide whether the latter has given informed consent. Informed consent has a specific meaning in GDPR (it must be freely given, specific, informed and unambiguous, opt-in and not opt-out, evidenced in writing etc).
Refresh marketing consents if necessary	If this is the legal ground that will be relied on, is it necessary to obtain a GDPR-compliant consent from the data subject? Who will be responsible?
Roll out new policies internally	Who will be responsible?
Implement destruction policy/destroy legacy records	Who will be responsible? What tasks, for example, need to be assigned to the IT team?
Training of staff on GDPR/new and altered policies	This is an all-pervasive topic. Compliance requires everyone in the business to understand the law, the internal policies, the duties to data subjects and what to do in the event of a data breach.

Ongoing compliance steps

The second step is a familiar theme in compliance; it is the need to remain vigilant about the response to the topic. Consider the following suggestions:

- Keep a watching brief on the guidance issued by both the ICO and from within the legal services industry. This has been a learning curve for all, including the thought leaders, and their thinking is filtering down to us in a fragmentary fashion. The ICO publishes a monthly online newsletter. Subscribing to this (via the ICO website, www.ico.org.uk) will give you alerts about additions to guidance, trends in their supervisory work and similar. The Law Society has also published its own downloadable guide to GDPR, available from www.lawsociety.org.uk. We also have risk resources from the SRA to help with our management and mitigation of hot spots such as cyber risks to information security.

- Ensure the topic is constantly part of your internal communications with your colleagues. It is essential that everyone understands the impact of misunderstandings. Remind them about the need to think beyond the duties owed to the clients of the firm; be clear about the scope of the data subject definition; be clear about what happens if they are talking to a third party that may fall into the category of a data processor; have confidence that they will have the correct conversations with data subjects, that they know who to discuss data subject requests and all other concerns with, and that anyone undertaking any form of marketing or publicity is responding to the GDPR implications safely.
- Ensure, therefore, that this topic is part of your induction exercises with new colleagues and that supervisors consider this to be part of their risk identification responsibilities.
- Keep a watching brief on the system adaptations and new processes that you have rolled out. Your objective in doing this work will have been to manage the risk of breaching the GDPR data protection principles. Do your processes help with this?
- Finally (for now), many firms have found that this topic has highlighted storage and destruction pinch points so that it is sensible to think about a project to tackle archived files and historic computer-based records. Also, now seems a good time to look again at file closure processes and ensure that the data you retain at this end of your relationship with your clients and other data subjects is not inconsistent with your GDPR policies.

Key points from Section 3

Essential knowledge to manage legal compliance
- SRA Standards and Regulations
- Legislation relevant to your business

Managing legal compliance in practice – the golden rules
- Identify the legislation that is relevant to your business.
- Ascertain those individuals who need to understand the importance of a particular law.
- Develop policies, systems and controls to normalise these topics.
- Assess your people's understanding of the topic.
- Develop strategies to plug knowledge gaps.
- Make training relevant and inclusive.
- Facilitate communication of concerns and queries.
- Roll out monitoring processes – are our responses appropriate and are our people compliant?
- Continue to monitor the law for external changes.
- Keep up to date with SRA interest in these topics.

Section 4:
Compliance tools and resources

Introduction

How comfortable would you feel if the SRA decided to visit your firm tomorrow?

In a book of this type, the author can steer the course for the reader and highlight the waypoints that require attention. What cannot be done is to produce any type of off-the-shelf solution that can be used by all readers as a shortcut to the correct position.

The reason for this is simple: having established the behaviours the firm must demonstrate, the onus is on the reader – whether they are a partner or in any sort of compliance or management role – to devise mechanisms to make the topic operational.

This requires buy-in to the notion that regulation, compliance and ethics must be demonstrated in modern law firms. All three topics are interdependent. The challenge in law firms is to facilitate the following:
- understanding what is involved in employing regulated people in an authorised law firm that is subject to regulatory oversight;
- demonstrating compliance with the regulatory position in such a way that an individual's right to practise, and the firm's right to remain authorised, is not questioned; and
- enabling the ethical response to be the norm.

Section 4: Compliance tools and resources

Acting ethically is more burdensome without the safety net of a compliance culture. Compliance is harder, sometimes impossible, to achieve without ethical behaviour. Neither of these will be convincing objectives without regulatory oversight, and regulatory standards are in jeopardy without compliance and ethics. In other words, these three topics form a perfect circle, or a perfect storm if things go awry.

This makes the life of a modern solicitor more interesting and the running of the modern law firm more dynamic than perhaps was previously the case.

Do not forget that the SRA is entitled to exercise supervisory functions and this may involve visits to your workplace as well as other forms of enquiry. It has the right to satisfy itself that your workplace is a safe environment. However, even a well-run firm may not have all the answers to these enquiries – there is no such thing as the perfect law firm, solicitor or employee. What the regulator will expect to see is a firm in which regulatory purpose is understood and compliance with regulatory standards is in evidence – and the glue that bonds everything together is ethical behaviour. These features will support the safe environment.

This concluding section includes a resources list, a brief summary of the SRA's proposals and some final offerings from a thought leader.

> "*Acting ethically is more burdensome without the safety net of a compliance culture. Compliance is harder, sometimes impossible, to achieve without ethical behaviour.*"

Chapter 12:
Be aware of recent changes

The SRA's first regulatory toolkit was known as the SRA Handbook. This was replaced on 25 November 2019 by the SRA Standards and Regulations which we have described in this book. There were many changes in the STaRs and it is important that the law firm, and everyone within it, works to the current replacements. So what's changed?

The highlights of the new regime are as follows:

- The SRA principles have been reduced from ten down to seven ethical requirements (including separate duties of honesty and integrity) to act
    - in a way that upholds the constitutional principle of the rule of law, and the proper administration of justice;
    - in a way that upholds the public trust and confidence in the solicitor's profession and in legal services provided by authorised persons;
    - with independence;
    - with honesty;
    - with integrity;
    - in a way that encourages equality, diversity and inclusion; and
    - in the best interests of each client.
- We now have two separate Codes of Conduct – one for solicitors

and the other for firms. Compliance officer duties are in the latter as are the law firm management requirements which were previously described in the Principles. The Code for Firms applies to all members of the law firm regardless of their status or position.
- The Accounts Rules have been simplified but in most respects we should be able to carry on as before.
- Solicitors are now entitled to carry out 'non-reserved' legal work within a business not regulated by a legal services regulator. Such solicitors are personally bound by the Code of Conduct for Solicitors, are not able to hold client money and are not required to have the equivalent professional indemnity insurance as authorised firms. They must also make clear to the users of their services exactly what protections are in place, including not providing access to the SRA Compensation Fund.
- Solicitors are also able to provide reserved legal services on a freelance basis, subject to certain conditions. Freelancers are not able to hold client money or employ staff and must have appropriate indemnity insurance. They must also explain to clients what regulatory protections apply.
- There is a new enforcement strategy, providing greater clarity on when and how the SRA would act against a firm or solicitor.

The following tables are based on tables from the SRA website[75] and show the transposition of the regulatory requirements and the current rules.

Table 17: Transposition of SRA requirements

Title	Retain, remove or combine with other rules?
SRA Practice Framework Rules 2011	Retain elements in each of the Individual and Firm Authorisation Regulations/Rules
SRA Practising Regulations 2011	
SRA Admission Regulations 2011	Replace with Individual Authorisation Regulations (and some elements in Education, Training and Assessment Provider Regulations)
SRA Higher Rights of Audience Regulations 2011	
SRA Quality Assurance Scheme for Advocates (Crime) Regulations 2013	
SRA Authorisation Rules 2011	Replace with Authorisation of Firms Rules
SRA Keeping of the Roll Regulations 2011	Retain but combine with other requirements in new Registers, Rolls and Information Regulations
SRA Training Regulations 2014 – Qualification and Provider Regulations	Combine some elements into Individual Authorisation Regulations; and some provisions retained to form new set of provider regulations
SRA Qualified Lawyers Transfer Scheme Regulations 2011	
SRA Suitability Test 2011	Retain a standalone document setting out rules for assessing character and suitability
SRA Indemnity Insurance Rules 2013	
SRA Indemnity Enactment Rules 2012	Retain (NB these rules are not included within phase two, but will be subject to separate consultation)
SRA Indemnity Rules 2012	
SRA Compensation Fund Rules 2011	

continued on next page

Section 4: Compliance tools and resources

Title	Retain, remove or combine with other rules?
SRA Intervention Powers (Statutory Trust) Rules 2011	Retain
SRA Disciplinary Procedure Rules 2011	Combine
SRA Cost of Investigations Regulations 2011	
SRA Overseas Rules 2013	Combine
SRA European Cross-border Practice Rules 2011	
SRA Property Selling Rules 2011	Remove
SRA Financial Services (Scope) Rules 2001	Retain
SRA Financial Services (Conduct of Business) Rules 2001	Retain

Table 18: The new SRA rules

Rules	What do they say?
SRA Principles	The ethical standards we expect of those we regulate
SRA Code of Conduct for Solicitors, RELs and RFLs	The professional standards and behaviours we expect of solicitors, RELs and RFLs in practice
SRA Code of Conduct for Firms	The responsibilities of authorised firms as regulated businesses
SRA Accounts Rules	How firms should keep their clients' money safe
SRA Education, Training and Assessment Provider Regulations	Our requirements for organisations providing education, training and delivering assessments to those seeking to be admitted as solicitors and beyond

continued on next page

Rules	What do they say?
SRA Assessment of Character and Suitability Rules	How we assess character and suitability of those seeking to join or be restored to the roll, to become authorised role-holders, or register as RFLs or RELs
SRA Authorisation of Individuals Regulations	Our requirements for individuals seeking authorisation as a solicitor, registered European lawyer or registered foreign lawyer
SRA Authorisation of Firms Rules	Our requirements relating to the authorisation of entities as recognised bodies, licensed bodies and recognised sole practices
SRA Application, Notice, Review and Appeal Rules	How we deal with applications and notifications made to us and our approach to reviews and appeals in relation to decisions we have made
SRA Registers, Roll and Information Regulations	What information we are required to keep about individuals and entities we authorise and other new information requirements
SRA Regulatory and Disciplinary Procedure Rules	How we investigate and take disciplinary and regulatory action for breaches of our rules and regulatory requirements
SRA Overseas Rules and Cross-border Practice Rules	How we regulate those providing legal services outside England and Wales, and what we expect from those engaged in cross-border practice
SRA Statutory Trust Rules	What we do with money we take possession of following an intervention into a practice
SRA Financial Services (Scope) Rules	Outlines the scope of the regulated financial services activities that may be undertaken by firms authorised by us and not regulated by the FCA
SRA Financial Services (Conduct of Business) Rules	How firms may carry on the regulated activities outlined in the SRA Financial Services (Scope) Rules, and the way firms that are dually regulated by us and the FCA may conduct their non-mainstream regulated activities
SRA Transparency Rules	The information that should be made available to clients and potential clients
SRA Glossary	Definitions of the terms used in our Handbook

Chapter 13:
Remote working – compliance considerations

Introduction
The premise of this book is that in order to have fuss-free careers and businesses, lawyers and law firms must accept that they need to have an appropriate understanding of, and response to, those who are required to regulate them or who are otherwise entitled to take an interest in what they do. In England and Wales we need to consider the Solicitors Regulation Authority and other stakeholder bodies including the Office for Legal Complaints, the Information Commissioner's Office, the National Crime Agency and similar external agencies.

The best lawyers and law firms understand that while relationships with clients are necessary for commercial success, the overriding motivation must be to demonstrate professionalism in practice. Clients come and go, new clients can always be won to replace those we might lose, but if we lose the confidence of our regulators and other agencies it is often a struggle to convince them to reinvest their trust.

Creating the correct culture
Law firm owners should aim to create the correct culture so that these regulatory concerns are addressed and evidenced, and so that ethical individual behaviour is properly fostered. Unfortunately, there are too

many examples of individuals falling short of the expected behaviours and being disciplined accordingly. Often these failings are entangled with the atmosphere of the workplace. Descriptions of "toxic environments" and "abominable working conditions" have made the headlines in the UK legal press in recent times and while this has not enabled the individual to avoid censure, the firms in question have also faced both regulatory and reputational criticism as a consequence. These reasons alone should provide sufficient justification for dealing with regulatory and ethical expectations properly.

In other words, the aim of everyone who owns a law firm, or is working in a law firm in a position of influence, should be to achieve an environment whereby compliance in practice is the business-as-usual position. In the workplace, this triggers the need to address a range of regulatory concerns:

- Do we have appropriate management of client relationships?
- Do we deal properly with issues arising from our role as officers of the court?
- Do we take seriously the protection of information, the avoidance of fraud or being used for fraudulent or otherwise illegal purposes?
- Do we use our knowledge and skillsets ethically?

No wonder there are so many policies, controls and procedures in modern law firms, and no wonder so many hire compliance professionals and otherwise create compliance resources to support business continuity.

Remote working – a new landscape

A very relevant and current observation is that the compliance experience and response is based on the premise that there is an office, a collective working space, where most managers and employees spend most of their time. The question to ask is whether this starting point remains fit for purpose if we consider the need for compliance responses to all types of challenges and, specifically, those connected to remote working.

In other words, while many of us are comfortable with colleagues, specifically fee-earning colleagues, having the occasional day out of the office and working from home, the consequence of this being the main place of work for the majority (if not all) staff for the foreseeable future must be considered now that 'self-isolation' and 'social distancing' are part of our vocabulary.

The impact of COVID-19

At the time of writing, we are in the midst of a lockdown triggered by the 2020 COVID-19 pandemic. Law firms across the globe have had to dust down their business continuity and disaster recovery plans and decide whether these are fit for purpose in circumstances that go far beyond the usual worst case scenarios of an IT outage or loss of a key individual or team. How does compliance work when there is no office? How does compliance work when no one else has an office? Looking beyond the global lockdown, what needs to happen in terms of compliance strategies if remote working becomes more commonplace now that our fee earners know that they can provide legal services without their daily commute and working from home becomes, as many commentators predict, the new normal?

What is clear with the benefit of hindsight is that the majority of our business continuity or disaster recovery plans, while often beautifully crafted documents, contain platitudes that don't quite cut the mustard when it comes to what we are now dealing with. 'Business as usual' is an aspirational phrase and, of course, commendable – but it does not capture the practical difficulties we are now encountering. A cynic might suggest that it has turned out to be somewhat hollow.

The new normal

Perhaps a more constructive approach is to consider those essential regulatory, compliance and ethical matters which the owners of the business and their compliance professionals cannot let slip in any circumstances. This new normal requires a changed response from compliance professionals in the business who will play a key role in ensuring that legal services can continue to be provided without compromising risk management and ethical behaviour standards.

Regardless of the end date of the 2020 pandemic, many commentators are already expressing the view that we will not revert to type as soon as the restrictions are lifted, and that the innovative use of technology has paved the way for continued remote or agile working. The lessons being learned, and the commentary from regulators and others who are responding to COVID-19, are helpful when developing new compliance polices, controls and procedures to accommodate working from home risk management.

Compliance as a science is dynamic. Policies and similar which are not regularly reviewed and refreshed are unlikely to be fit for purpose; compliance responses must be agile and deal with changing circumstances while ensuring that standards are not able to slip below a safe baseline position. In March 2020, the SRA expressed its requirements in a series of coronavirus communications with the following starting statement on its approach to compliance:[76]

We expect solicitors and firms to continue to meet the high standards the public expect. This means they must do everything they reasonably can to comply with our rules, and follow our Principles. This includes serving the best interests of their clients and upholding the rule of law.

We expect firms to have appropriate contingency plans in place for disruption, but we recognise that these are exceptional circumstances and the coming months could present particularly challenging issues.

We must all remain pragmatic. We will take a proportionate approach: this includes our approach to enforcement. If we do receive complaints, we would take into account mitigating circumstances, as set out in our enforcement strategy. This includes focusing on serious misconduct, and clearly distinguishing between people who are trying to do the right thing, and those who are not.

We would recommend that if you do face compliance difficulties linked to the virus, you should clearly document the approach you have taken.

In other words, regardless of our working environment, the regulator's expectations are as follows:
- Standards of service will not slip.
- Contingency plans will have been drawn.
- A pragmatic attitude on the part of both regulator and regulated should prevail.

If 2020 is the year when traditional working practices change then the compliance function must ensure that it adapts to manage regulatory concerns. The starting point must be to consider how to deliver the message that the needs of managers and employees are being considered and that different needs are being supported.

This might seem counterintuitive to many lawyers who would tend towards a client-centric response to changed circumstances. However, if justification is needed for this colleagues-first approach, then the SRA Code of Conduct for Firms describes the proper governance standards that should be maintained (at chapter 2) and notes (at chapter 4) the service and competence standards in respect of the needs of staff.

By way of example, consider the following paragraphs:[77]

2.1 You have effective governance structures, arrangements, systems and controls in place that ensure:

(a) you comply with all the SRA's regulatory arrangements, as well as with other regulatory and legislative requirements, which apply to you;

(b) your managers and employees comply with the SRA's regulatory arrangements which apply to them;

(c) your managers and interest holders and those you employ or contract with do not cause or substantially contribute to a breach of the SRA's regulatory arrangements by you or your managers or employees;

(d) your compliance officers are able to discharge their duties under paragraphs 9.1 and 9.2 below.

2.2 You keep and maintain records to demonstrate compliance with your obligations under the SRA's regulatory arrangements.

2.3 You remain accountable for compliance with the SRA's regulatory arrangements where your work is carried out through others, including your managers and those you employ or contract with.

2.4 You actively monitor your financial stability and business viability. Once you are aware that you will cease to operate, you effect the orderly wind-down of your activities.

[...]

4.3 You ensure that your managers and employees are competent to carry out their role, and keep their professional knowledge and skills, as well as understanding of their legal, ethical and regulatory obligations, up to date.

4.4 You have an effective system for supervising clients' matters.

Remote working should not – whether for regulatory, commercial or reputational reasons – be allowed to compromise these standards.

KEY QUESTIONS

- What messages are we communicating to our colleagues about the support they will receive from the firm?
- Are the correct people delivering these key messages (ie, are we demonstrating that standards of behaviour are endorsed by the owners and other senior colleagues)?
- Are we reminding our colleagues of the expectations which the business has of them as ambassadors for the brand?
- Are we recognising that not everyone will adapt comfortably to remote working and are we fulfilling employment duties to protect the wellbeing and mental health of our colleagues? Does that mean that colleagues from the human resources team should contribute? Could we facilitate learning in these different ways of working and in mental health and wellbeing?

- Are the right people visible and accessible? Are the owners of the business, the COLP and COFA, money laundering reporting officer and senior lawyers and supervisors available to support colleagues? Also, do these individuals have the necessary access to support for themselves?
- Are we being clear about the essential compliance messages that remain non-negotiable despite the circumstances?
- Are we also being clear about what we expect in terms of notification and reporting duties?
- What do we consider to be the new business as usual in terms of the provision of legal services?

Compliance processes and procedures cannot be allowed to decline or become less relevant in new normal, non-office-centric, ways. Think about just some of the considerations, for example, that are included within the duty to demonstrate effective governance structures. We still need to incept new matters, new clients, and new matters for old clients in a risk-managed way. This requires maintenance of client identification processes for both SRA regulatory purposes (ie, paragraph 8.1 of the SRA Code of Conduct for Solicitors, mirrored in the SRA Code of Conduct for Firms) and anti-money laundering legal requirements, as well as risk analysis by the correct people.

Client identification and care

Short-term considerations
The immediate issue with meeting the standards is this: if more clients are self-isolating, how do you manage the risks that this presents in terms of the client identification checks that are necessary?

While email usage will ease the way we act on client instructions, the risk of never meeting a client face-to-face will need to be managed, perhaps by the use of FaceTime or similar. Legal duties cannot be compromised; it should not be forgotten that where services are subject to the Money Laundering Regulations there is a legal obligation to perform customer due diligence in a risk-appropriate way. Not seeing clients face-to-face automatically triggers the need for enhanced due diligence and additional, albeit alternative, identification and verification methods.

The longer term

The more long-term considerations include the need to ensure that client identification is achieved consistently, notwithstanding remote working practices. This provokes decisions about what functions should remain centralised and even office-based. Most firms have file-opening processes that are a combination of fee earner acquired knowledge plus support staff contributions, and this generally works well to ensure that compliance requirements are risk managed. If the fee earners are working remotely, systems need to adapt to ensure that identification duties are captured.

The other important compliance elements of client onboarding are of course conflicts checks plus the delivery of appropriate client care. Taking on new clients must be a conflicts-assessed decision regardless of external circumstances, whether these are a lockdown situation or just a new way of working. Failure to identify either own interest or client conflicts will involve the individual concerned in a fundamental ethical mistake and could well have regulatory and reputational consequences for the firm.

Client care information must be given to clients and must be appropriate to their needs and accurately reflect the services to be delivered. If services are delivered remotely then consideration must be given to the appropriateness of the standard letter. Who else will be available if the fee earner is not responding? How can the fee earner be contacted? What are the service standard commitments?

We also need to deliver messages about the need for the firm to demonstrate that it is keeping records for regulatory and compliance purposes. Mistakes will continue to be made and complaints received.

Records must be maintained about regulatory breaches. Put bluntly, the firm will be on the back foot with the SRA, the Legal Ombudsman and their insurers if these are not handled correctly and notified promptly.

Risk management

The dynamic response
Another important message from the compliance team must be about the approach to the management of risk events and the decisions that should be made by the senior members of the firm. This is made necessary by the SRA Code of Conduct for Firms, paragraph 2.5: "You identify, monitor and manage all material risks to your business."

This phrasing indicates that a dynamic response to risk is required with risk decisions being kept under review at all times. With rapid changes in working arrangements, and the impact of lockdown, the firm's risk register and supporting documentation should be reviewed and mitigation measures assessed for appropriateness. Some firms might consider it appropriate to introduce a Coronavirus Task Force or similar to lead the firm's response to the regulatory, ethical and compliance challenges.

Knowing your risks
Only you will know the specific risks that your business model attracts. In previous chapters we have seen that there is a need to consider risks triggered by your client base, your work streams, your people and similar. Over and above this, the COVID-19 pandemic has created risks that are more general in scope. In particular, all firms need to consider data protection risks, cyber and other frauds, risks to client money protection, loss of staff, and financial and business viability considerations. Some of these risks would need to continue to be analysed should remote working become the new normal.

By way of example, remote working will expose the business to different confidentiality and data breach issues, so consideration is

"Water cooler conversations still need to happen regardless of circumstances."

required about case management, access to paper-based files, storage and destruction of paper-based documentation, IT usage and the risk of cyber-attack.

It is a sad observation that we are being made aware of cyber scammers taking advantage of COVID-19, and law firms are unlikely to be immune from such attacks. The risk response must be that appropriate mitigation is put in place to lessen the risks of an ethical or legal breach of duty. The SRA has suggested introducing measures such as providing limited information to colleagues who do not usually work at home and/or do not have access to secure IT or adequate equipment, and providing details of the arrangements that have been introduced.

Supervision

Effective supervision must be maintained regardless of working environment. Arguably, good supervision and the behaviours of supervisory staff will be key to a successful transition to this new style of work.

Supervisors who understand that their role is to be the lynchpin between individuals and the business as a whole are invaluable assets. This should not come as a surprise, but the new challenge is to deliver the right messages about supervision in the current climate and to ensure that solicitors and other regulated lawyers who must comply with the SRA Code of Conduct for Solicitors, including registered European lawyers and registered foreign lawyers, remember the individual regulatory duties placed on them by paragraph 3.5:[78]

Where you supervise or manage others providing legal services:
(a) you remain accountable for the work carried out through them; and
(b) you effectively supervise work being done for clients.

This individual responsibility is a demanding expectation at the best of times, but the role-holder can take comfort from the fact that they are supported by paragraph 4.1 in the Code of Conduct for Firms which requires the business to have "an effective system for supervising clients' matters".[79]

The best supervisors are the individuals who are visible, accessible, unflappable and diligent. These skills are as important as ever but need to be coupled with the need to be adaptable, to be available via telephone or video conference facilities, and to consider the particular needs of colleagues requiring support commensurate with their experience or – perhaps more pertinently – lack of experience. Consider the needs of trainee solicitors, paralegals and other less experienced colleagues who have been pushed into a new way of working which might not be appropriate given the skillsets they currently possess. Water cooler conversations still need to happen regardless of circumstances.

Other considerations
In terms of dealing with client matters more generally, we have already mentioned conflicts and confidentiality. Consideration also needs to be given to how we demonstrate that we are acting on clients' instructions that are given properly, and/or the properly authorised instructions of third parties, by:
- monitoring and properly recording undertakings;
- protecting client money;
- upholding the right behaviours in terms of equality, diversity and inclusion; and
- ensuring our duties to the court are not compromised.

These are strange times dictating an immediate response, but more permanent changes to our ways of working must also be discussed. Compliance professionals have always been at the centre of business continuity and this continues to be the case.

Chapter 14: Conclusion

To help consolidate and reinforce the messages outlined in the previous thirteen chapters, here are some concluding thoughts contributed by another subject expert.

INSIDER'S INSIGHT

Helen Carr is a risk and compliance consultant who has previously worked with the SRA as a senior ethics adviser and a practice standards unit adviser and has also worked within the Law Society's Risk and Compliance Service as a consultant.

What makes a bad law firm a bad law firm?
Most lawyers do not start out with the intention that they will be bad at what they do. Of course, there is a small contingent of individuals who either started out dishonest, or who became dishonest along the way. This contribution is not so concerned with those people, and instead we will take a broader look at those firms set up by honest practitioners with a desire to succeed. What are some of the indicators as to whether they will be successful or will fail? Why are some firms successful and profitable and others struggle to stay afloat?

The reasons for some firms' success and others' failure can be complex and varied – the areas of law practised; the local economic conditions; the availability of quality personnel; the availability of appropriate business premises; and the type of client base will all have an impact. Many of these factors are outside the control of the law firm but there is a key determiner, within the control of all law firms, which can impact significantly on a firm's ability to succeed – its approach to regulatory compliance.

Done well, a firm's compliance infrastructure can aid and enhance all aspects of a firm. Beyond this, it is an essential tool to ensure a sound ethos for the business.

So, what does a good compliance infrastructure look like? The answer to this question will, to some extent, depend on factors including the size of the firm; the range of services offered; the hierarchical structure; and the type of client base. However, there are key building blocks that, laid well, will help to ensure a solid foundation, notwithstanding the variables mentioned above. These are:

- how the firm manages risk;
- monitoring and protecting the firm's financial stability;
- the approach to anti-money laundering compliance;
- how the firm looks after clients' money and assets, including its approach to data protection and cyber security; and
- the approach to supervision and management.

We will look further into each of these areas and we will consider practical steps firms can take to enhance their performance. Whilst these are not the only subjects to consider for a firm's regulatory compliance portfolio, a robust approach in each of these will go a long way to forming a sound base on which to build other compliance structures.

Risk management

In terms of regulation of lawyers in England and Wales, the concept of risk management has been a fairly recent phenomenon. In the last *decade or so, we have seen an increased emphasis from the main legal regulator, SRA, on managing risk – both for the regulator and for the regulated community. In the wider non-legal commercial sphere, this is not news – many businesses have operated risk registers to monitor and evaluate risk, and have appointed named individuals to fill the role of risk manager, for several decades.*

This is not to say that legal practices have been oblivious to the benefits of risk awareness and management until it was listed as a priority requirement by the SRA. All good businesses, both legal and non-legal, have a keen awareness of risks and threats to their continuity, the services they provide and the work they carry out.

As we look at the various compliance areas listed above we will consider how each will also fall within the general category of risk management. Typically, firms that fail have not engaged with the risk management process and, in particular, have not provided for systems and processes to manage risks in the areas set out below.

Financial stability

Market conditions can fluctuate and what were once profitable areas of law can suddenly become unprofitable. An example of this is the proposed changes to civil litigation in the area of personal injury claims in England and Wales. Another example would be the impact on real estate practices of the financial crash in 2008 and the subsequent recession. Firms practising in these areas have seen a real impact on their profitability and have had to consider moving into new and diverse areas of practice to survive.

A firm in financial difficulty can also pose a risk to client money: the SRA identified in research documented in 2014 that "[i]n over a quarter of cases [of firms in financial difficulty], evidence of misuse or misappropriation of client money was found".[80] *For these reasons, monitoring and protecting the financial stability of a law firm is a fundamental risk requirement. Practical steps identified by the SRA in its 2014 report that firms can take to manage this risk include:*

- *making improvements to accounts procedures and reconciliation of accounts;*
- *reducing office space to reduce rental costs;*
- *chasing outstanding payments for completed work and improved management of work in progress (WIP); and*
- *recruitment of fee earners to facilitate diversification into new market areas.*

Other examples of good practice they identify include:
- *effective business and debt planning;*
- *assessment of future performance;*
- *restructuring of debt repayments; and*
- *improving accounting procedures.*

At its core, properly managing and providing for your firm's financial stability will ensure longevity and agility in a variety of market conditions.

Anti-money laundering compliance
This is a huge subject area and one which is deserving of its own publication. The intention in covering it here is to highlight key areas of compliance and good practice evidenced by those firms with a robust approach to compliance. In contrast, firms who have encountered regulatory and legal difficulties in this area tend to be those with poor systems, and with an inadequately trained staff base.

Key systems and requirements include:
- a documented process for verifying the identity of your client, whether corporate or individual;
- a trained staff base that understands the necessity of knowing your client, and the ability to check and verify their details and information using a range of resources including the use of sanctions lists;
- having a named person within the firm with overall

responsibility for implementing and reviewing the firm's systems and procedures, and with responsibility for reporting matters to the appropriate law enforcement agency when necessary; and
- periodically reviewing the firm's risk profile and the efficacy of its systems and procedures.

With the sanctions relating to involvement in money laundering being legal as well as regulatory, and with the ultimate sanction being a loss of liberty, it is vital that this risk area is provided for and mitigated by the firm's systems. The practical implications of getting it wrong are not just individual consequences, but also consequences for society as a whole – organised crime and the funding of terrorist activities are real risks where money laundering is concerned.

Clients' money and assets, data protection and cyber security

It is a fundamental part of the role of being a lawyer that you are able to protect clients' legitimate assets and money. This responsibility is constantly under challenge from new and emerging threats, particularly in the area of cyber-crime. This is an area of crime that has increased dramatically over the last five years or so, and law firms are prime targets for criminals. We have already seen a range of scams and attacks specifically aimed at law firms: major targets are those firms involved in property transactions due to the significant sums of money they hold.

It is likely that, unless you have a particular expertise in information technology and systems, you will need some third-party assistance to ensure that you have up-to-date protection from cyber-attacks. However, as the weakest link in any cyber security system is a human operator, there are steps that firms can take to mitigate their exposure to risk in this area. These include:
- training all staff to understand how a cyber-attack can be made and what steps they can take to protect themselves and the firm;
- keeping up to date with the various types of attack and scam used;

- *having a robust and secure IT infrastructure;*
- *ensuring that the firm is properly protected with appropriate insurance cover; and*
- *having appropriate policies for the use of emails and the internet, and monitoring the implementation of these policies.*

In 2018, the UK Government identified that a considerable number of businesses in the UK had been subject to a cyber-attack.[81] The majority of respondents to the governmental survey indicated that their staff had received fraudulent emails. This highlights the importance of having a strong and comprehensive response to this threat including a well-trained workforce.

Supervision and management

At the core of any properly run and successful business is a good governance structure and an appropriate managerial hierarchy. It is essential that those in a position of management know and understand what is happening within the firm, and consequently what are its strengths and areas of weakness. This information can help with both short- and long-term business planning and forecasting.

A good supervisory structure will also help to ensure that any mistakes or problems are identified as early as possible, with the best opportunity for remedial or mitigatory actions to be taken. It helps a firm's personnel to feel valued and secure, and it can help with staff attrition rates.

Suggestions for inclusion in a firm's approach to supervision are:
- Periodic reviews of individuals' files or matters. This can help with personal development and will assist in the identification of potential problem areas. Conversely, such file reviews can also shine a light on areas of good practice and individual strengths that can be used for the benefit of the firm as a whole.
- Regular one-to-one meetings with the firm's personnel. It is often those who are immersed in the substantive work of the firm who

are best placed to identify risks to the firm at an early stage. In addition, the benefits of an opportunity for a direct and holistic conversation about an individual's work area can include identifying opportunities for development, and the ability to tackle any problems or grievances at an early stage.
- *The recording of key data arising from file reviews and other supervisory mechanisms to enable senior management to have a broad overview of the firm's status in certain areas. This can help with budget planning and forecasting and overall risk management.*

Knowing and understanding what is going on within your firm places you in a strong position to react and to adapt to threats and risks as they emerge. It also helps you to understand where best to place your resources and how to invest in your firm and its personnel to ensure maximum effectiveness.

Concluding comments

In this contribution we have considered a broad range of areas that should form part of any firm's regulatory risk and compliance plan. Strong systems in these areas will help to ensure a healthy and robust approach that can be adapted to suit a variety of external conditions. It should be noted that whilst these areas are fundamental to any plan, they should not be considered to the exclusion of other important subjects such as, for example, client care and complaints handling; the identification and management of conflicts of interest; and legal professional privilege and the duties of confidentiality and disclosure.

The legal regulatory authority in each jurisdiction will have its own rules and requirements and it is of paramount importance that practitioners are familiar with these and understand the framework in which they are operating. Firms that fail almost universally do not understand and comply with these requirements.

Chapter 15: Resources

It is essential that law firm owners, managers and staff keep up to date with regulatory thinking. This requires an understanding of the evolutionary nature of such thinking. Below are some current resources and sources of help.

Useful websites

SRA website – www.sra.org.uk
Law Society website – www.lawsociety.org.uk
Law Society Gazette – www.lawgazette.co.uk
Legal Services Board – www.legalservicesboard.org.uk
Office for Legal Complaints – www.legalombudsman.org.uk
Information Commissioner's Office – www.ico.org.uk

Useful resources

From the SRA

SRA Update e-newsletter
Compliance News, the COLP and COFA e-newsletter
Risk Outlook

Risk resources
Warning notices
Scam alerts
Guidance articles
Ethics helpline service

From the Law Society
Advice and practice notes
Anti-money laundering resources
Data protection resources
Practice advice helpline service
Risk and compliance service

Notes

1. www.sra.org.uk/solicitors/standards-regulations/.
2. www.sra.org.uk/sra/news/press/handbook-reforms-june-2018.page.
3. SDT case number 11717-2017.
4. www.sra.org.uk/sra/corporate-strategy/risk-framework/risk-faqs/.
5. *Ibid.*
6. www.sra.org.uk/risk/outlook/risk-outlook-2019-2020/.
7. SDT Case Number 11730-2017.
8. SDT Case Number 11619-2017.
9. SDT Case number 11599-2017.
10. www.sra.org.uk/risk/risk-resources/information-security-report/.
11. www.sra.org.uk/solicitors/guidance/warning-notices/holiday-sickness-claims--warning-notice/.
12. In this book, the terms 'partner' and 'partnership' are used to describe not just partners, but directors, members and sole practitioners.
13. *Wingate and Evans v SRA; SRA v Malins* [2018] EWCA Civ 366.
14. www.sra.org.uk/solicitors/code-of-conduct/guidance/question-of-ethics.page.
15. SDT Case number 11657-2017.
16. www.sra.org.uk/solicitors/resources/cpd/competence-statement/.
17. https://lplc.com.au.
18. SRA Authorisation Rules 2011, rule 8.2.
19. SRA Authorisation Rules 2011, rule 8.5.
20. This report is no longer available on the SRA website.
21. Legal Services Act 2007, section 1(2).
22. SRA Principles 2011, rule 2.1.
23. www.sra.org.uk/sra/decision-making/guidance/general-dishonesty/.
24. www.sra.org.uk/solicitors/guidance/ethics-guidance/acting-with-integrity/.
25. www.sra.org.uk/solicitors/guidance/ethics-guidance/guidance-on-the-sra-s-approach-to-equality-diversity-and-inclusion/.
26. www.sra.org.uk/solicitors/standards-regulations/principles/.
27. This report is no longer available on the SRA website.
28. *Alastair Brett v Solicitors Regulation Authority* (SRA) [2014] EWHC 2974.
29. Steven Vaughan & Emma Oakley, "'Gorilla exceptions' and the ethically apathetic corporate lawyer", *Legal Ethics* (2016) vol 19, no. 1, pp50–75.
30. *Ibid.*
31. www.sra.org.uk/solicitors/resources/cpd/competence-statement/.
32. Included within the Statement of Solicitor Competence and from the definition provided in M Eraut and B Boulay, "Developing the Attributes of Medical Professional Judgement and Competence", University of Sussex, 2000.
33. www.sra.org.uk/risk/outlook/risk-outlook-2017-2018.

Notes

34 www.sra.org.uk/solicitors/standards-regulations/principles/.
35 SRA Code of Conduct for Solicitors, paragraph 6.1.
36 SRA Code of Conduct for Solicitors, paragraph 6.2.
37 SRA Code of Conduct for Solicitors, paragraph 5.
38 SRA Code of Conduct for Solicitors, paragraph 2.
39 SRA Code of Conduct for firms, paragraph 2.5.
40 SRA Authorisation of Firms Rules, Rule 1.1.
41 There is a narrow exception in a company group structure where a recognised body has a subsidiary company which is a licensed body, that has less than 10% non-lawyer ownership. See Legal Services Act 2007, s 72.
42 *Andrew Michael Tilbury* (STD 9880-2008), paragraphs 86–87.
43 *Jane Robinson* (SDT 9365-2005), paragraphs 179–180.
44 *Philip Joseph Shiner* (STD 11510-2016), paragraph 94.14.
45 www.sra.org.uk/solicitors/guidance/ethics-guidance/acting-with-integrity/.
46 SDT Case number 11749-2017.
47 www.kingsleynapley.co.uk/insights/blogs/legal-services-regulation-blog/the-quality-of-integrity-a-review-of-the-court-of-appeals-decision-in-wingate-and-evans-v-sra-sra-v-malins-2018-ewca-civ-366-in-the-context-of-legal-services-regulation.
48 [2017] EWHC 835 (Admin).
49 [2018] EWCA Civ 366.
50 [2017] EWHC 411 (Admin).
51 [1994] 1 WLR 512.
52 [2017] EWHC 210 (Admin).
53 Richard Simmons, "Revealed: The scale of sexual harassment in law", *The Lawyer*, March 2018. Available at: www.thelawyer.com/metoo-lawyers-sexual-harassment-survey-2018-2/.
54 Now SRA Principle 2 in the SRA Standards and Regulations.
55 *Ibid*.
56 www.sra.org.uk/solicitors/guidance/warning-notices/risk-factors-in-personal-injury-claims--warning-notice/.
57 www.sra.org.uk/solicitors/guidance/warning-notices.
58 www.sra.org.uk/risk/risk-resources/balancing-duties-litigation/.
59 www.lawsociety.com.au/practising-law-in-NSW/ethics-and-compliance/regulatory-compliance.
60 As an example of this difference in philosophy see Alice Woolley's article in the Canadian online legal magazine *SLAW*. Available at: www.slaw.ca/author/woolley/.
61 www.supremecourt.uk/docs/lord-neuberger-121115-speech.pdf.
62 See Department for Business Innovation and Skills, Better Regulation Delivery Office, "Ethical Business Regulation: Understanding the Evidence", February 2016.
63 For a fuller development of this point see the article, "The End of Leverage" on the Adam Smith Esq website. Available at: https://adamsmithesq.com/2017/11/the-end-of-leverage/.
64 "Losing the Plot; Residential conveyancing complaints and their causes." Available at: www.legalombudsman.org.uk.
65 www.sra.org.uk/sra/how-we-work/reports/first-tier-complaints/.
66 SDT Case number 11758-2017.
67 Examples include SDT Case number 11625-2017 (anti-Semitic posts on a Facebook account).
68 No longer available on the SRA website.
69 www.sra.org.uk/risk/outlook/risk-outlook-2019-2020/.
70 www.nationalcrimeagency.gov.uk/publications/suspicious-activity-reports-sars/826-suspicious-activity-reports-annual-report-2017/file.
71 *R v (1) Griffiths (2) Pattison* [2006] EWCA Crim 2155.
72 *Fuglers & Ors v SRA* [2014] EWHC 179 (Admin) (QB).
73 www.anti-moneylaundering.org/AboutAML.aspx#Guide.
74 This post from the ICO blog is widely reported but no longer available online.
75 By kind permission of SRA.
76 www.sra.org.uk/sra/news/coronavirus-update.
77 www.sra.org.uk/solicitors/standards-regulations/code-conduct-firms/.
78 www.sra.org.uk/solicitors/standards-regulations/code-conduct-solicitors/.
79 www.sra.org.uk/solicitors/standards-regulations/code-conduct-firms/.

Notes

80 Solicitors Regulation Authority, "Steering the Course: Research into the characteristics and risks associated with law firms in financial difficulty", February 2014. Available at: www.sra.org.uk/risk/risk-resources/risks-and-financial-difficulty/.

81 UK Government, Department for Digital, Culture, Media and Sport, Cyber Security Breaches Survey 2018. Available at: www.gov.uk/government/statistics/cyber-security-breaches-survey-2018.

About the author

Tracey Calvert
Director, Oakalls Consultancy Limited
tcalvert@oakallsconsultancy.co.uk

Tracey is a lawyer and the director of Oakalls Consultancy Limited. She is a regulatory, compliance and ethics specialist providing a variety of advisory services to members of the solicitor's profession.

She is a regular speaker and trainer on these topics and has delivered presentations both within the UK and internationally.

She is currently the co-vice-chair of the International Bar Association's Professional Ethics Committee and a board member of both the Wilmington Group's Legal Compliance Association and the Law Society's *Legal Compliance Bulletin*.

She is a contributor to *Cordery on Legal Services* and has written several books on compliance and ethics. Full details are available at www.oakallsconsultancy.co.uk.

Tracey was previously employed by the Law Society and the SRA as a senior ethics adviser and a policy executive. She has also worked both in private practice and in an in-house role.

Index

Page references to Tables are in *italics*.

Administration of Justice Act 1985, *170*
Advertising Standards Agency, 171
advocacy, 131–132
    regulatory expectations, 132–133, *132–133*
    spoken and written, 111
alternative business structure, 73, 136
anti-money laundering, 39, 167, 230–231
    see also **money laundering**
audit trail, 117

benefits of compliance, 70–71
Black Norman Solicitors, 42
Brett, Alastair, 94–95
Bribery Act 2010, *173*

Carr, Helen, 227–233
character, 82
client care, 78, *101*, 121–122
    at the end of retainer, 128–129
    informing about change of fee earner/supervisor, 127–128
    remote working, 222
client identification, 122
    remote working, 221–222
    sameness during the course, 127
    satisfaction about, 124
client inception, 121–122
    client conflict, 125
    conflicts of interest, 125, 127
    continuous monitoring, 127–128
    financial information, 128
    information sharing and disclosure, 125–126
    material information and confidentiality, 125
    relationship, beginning of, 122–126
    retainer, 125, 128–129
    standard of service, 126
client relationship, 112, 122–126
clients
    see also **client care; client identification; client inception**
    instruction capacity, 122–124
    intake, 191
    laws applied on behalf of, 171–172
    money and assets of, 231–232
    protecting and promoting the interest of, 14–15
    requirement, understanding of, 124
Clyde & Co LLP, 22–23
colleagues
    communicating correct messages to, 147–149
    confidence in principles of, 95–96
commitment to regulation, compliance and ethics, 63
communication skills, 112, 191–192
Companies Act, *171*
competencies, 109
    definition of, 108
    Statement of Solicitor Competence *see* **Statement of Solicitor Competence**
    of supervisors, 51–52
complaints
    definition of, 155–156
    process, 55
    and regulatory policy and disciplinary work, 11–13

Index

complaints handler, 46
compliance, 13, 169, 206
  checklist, *170–171*
  definition of, 6
  evidence of *see* **evidence of compliance**
  laws applied on behalf of clients, 171–172
  with legal obligations *see* **legal obligations**
  legislation, 172, *173–175*
  pinch points and strategies, *58–59*
  practice-related laws, 169–171
  records, 118
  and systems and process addition, 56–57
  turning into business opportunity, 190
compliance management, 68–70
compliance officer, 144, 210
  ethics, 43
  role in governance structure, 40–44, 50
compliance officer for finance and administration (COFA), 41, 42, 43, 44, 46, 47, 60, 62, 221
  case study, 42
compliance officer for legal practice (COLP), 40–41, 42, 43, 44, 46, 47, 60, 62, 169, 221
compliance professionals, role in governance structure, 46–53, 60, 62, 169, 221
confidentiality, *102–103*, 107, 128
conflicts of interest, *102*, 107, 125, 127
consultants, 48
consumers *see* **clients**
conveyancing services, 157, 182
corporate social responsibility, 152
court duties, *103*
Courts and Legal Services Act 1990, *170*
COVID-19 pandemic, 217
  SRA's approach to compliance, 218–219
  remote working *see* **remote working**
Criminal Finances Act 2017, *174–175*, 182, 186
critical thinking, 110
cyber-crime, 23, 225, 231–232
cyber scamming, 225

data protection, 23, 128, 167, 197, 231–232
  see also **information security**
  basic knowledge, 198–199
  General Data Protection Regulation, 198–203
  responsibility of, 197–198
Data Protection Act 2018, *175*, 198
data protection officer, role in governance structure, 45
disciplinary decisions, 16, 20, 22, 49
disclosure duties, *102–103*, 107

documentation
  management documentation of policies, 117
  of office systems and processes, 54, 56–57
  related to training programmes, 117–118
  risk analysis documentation, 118
drafts preparation, 111, 120

effective governance, 25–27
  see also **proper governance**
  and remote working, 221
  reporting lines, 27, *27–30*
effective law firm management, 11–17, 91–92
employee-centred approaches, 55
employment mix, 59
Equality Act 2010, *101*, *173*
Esparraga, Francisco, 81–83
essential behaviour, 85–114
  confidence in colleagues' principles, 95–96
  SRA Code of Conduct 2019, 96–107
  SRA Principles 2019, 86–95
  Statement of Solicitor Competence *see* **Statement of Solicitor Competence**
ethical service, commercial benefits of, 148–149
ethics, ethical behaviour, 81, 149–152, 206
  definition of, 6
  Francisco Esparraga's insight on, 81–83
evidence of compliance, 115–120
  audit trail, 117
  documentation, 117–118
  policies in official manual, *118–119*
  policy drafting, 120

face-to-face meeting, with clients, 221
factors of successful compliance culture, 67–68
facts, relevancy, 110
fee earner, 222
file audits, 55
file-opening process, 222
Financial Action Task Force, 184
financial risk management, 148, 191
Financial Services and Markets Act 2000, *173–174*
financial stability, 229–230
freelance legal services, 210
Fuglers LLP, 183–184

Galza, Katherine, 140–144
General Data Protection Regulation, *175*, 198–199
  checklist, *200–202*
  ongoing steps, 202–203
  strategies to manage, 199

Index

good business practice, application of, 114
governance *see* effective governance; proper governance
Graham, Christopher, 198

Harvie, Nigel, 75–78
heads of department, role in governance structure, 40
HM Revenue & Customs (HMRC), 183–184
Hodges, Christopher, 151
honesty, 108–109
Howdle, Christopher, 20, 22

independence, 134, 135–137
 compromise of, 137
 definition of, 135
 in SRA Standards and Regulations, 136–137
Information Commissioner's Office (ICO), 198, 202
information security, 23, 128
see also data protection
insurance distribution officer, role in governance structure, 45
integrity, 82, 108–109, 134, 139–140

law firms
 bad law firm, 227–233
 challenges, 205
 financial stability, 15
 governance structure, 15
  see also effective governance; proper governance
 management of, 219
 and remote working *see* remote working
 risks, 15
 role-holders *see under* proper governance
 work culture, 215–216
Law Society of England and Wales, 153
Law Society of New South Wales, 148–149
Legal Aid, Sentencing and Punishment of Offenders Act 2012, 172
Legal Complaints Service, 153
legal counsel, role in governance structure, 38–40
legal knowledge, 109, 172
legal obligations, 165–167
 case study, 165–166
Legal Ombudsman *see* Ombudsman
Legal Practitioners' Liability Committee (LPLC), 54
legal research, 110
Legal Services Act 2007, 6, 11, 14, 86, 153, *170*
Legal Services Board, 11

Limited Liability Partnership Act, *171*
litigation, 131–132
 independence in, 134, 135–137
 integrity in, 134, 139–144
 regulatory expectations, 132–133, *132–133*
 risk pinch points and strategies, 144–146
Locke Lord (UK) LLP, 14, 16

mail monitoring, 55
management documentation, of policies, 117
management expectations, of colleagues, 120
management team, role in governance structure, 37–38, 50
managerial decisions policies, 117
Miller, Iain, 149–152
money laundering, 22–23, 177
 basic knowledge, 186
 case studies, 22–23, 183–184
 Emma Oettinger's insight, 190–193
 'relevant' business, 186–187
 risk prioritisation, 179–184
 and sanctions, 193–194
 strategies to demonstrate compliance, 186–189
 UK's target, 177
Money Laundering Regulations, 180, 186, 222
 compliance checklist, *187–189*
money laundering reporting officer, 45
morality, 82

National Crime Agency (NCA), 180
negotiation, 111
new entrants, 13
nominated officer, role in governance structure, 45
non-mandatory compliance resources, 46–47
non-solicitors, 59–62, 92, 172

Oakley, Emma, 95, 106
Oettinger, Emma
 on money laundering, 190–193
 on sanctions, 194–195
Office for Professional Body AML Supervision (OPBAS), 181
Office for the Supervision of Solicitors, 153
Office of Legal Complaints (OLC), 153
Ombudsman, 115, 122, 125, 153–154
 lessons learned from, 157–160
 reports by, 157–160
 and Solicitors Regulation Authority, 154–155, 158
 strategies for management of, 155–157
organised crime, 179, 181–182

245

Index

Panama Papers, 184
Paradise Papers, 184
partners, role in governance structure, 30–37
   consensual approach, *31–35*
   Pelopidas on, 36–37
partnership commitment to compliance objectives, 66
Pelopidas, Alexander, 36–37
personal diary-keeping, 120
Philip, Paul, 6–7
Pickard, Stephen, 165–166
planning, 112
policies
   contained in office manual, 118, *118–119*
   drafting, 120
   management documentation, 117
   managerial decisions, 117
positions descriptions for employees, 54
practice management tools, 54–55
practice managers, 169
practice-related laws, 169–171
problem solving, 110
Proceeds of Crime Act 2002, *174*, 181, 186
professional principles
   and SRA's regulatory toolkit, 86–95
   in terms of Legal Services Act 2007, 86
professionalism, 108–110, 215
proper governance, 27–30, 87
   see also effective governance
   case study, 42
   compliance officers, 40–44
   compliance professionals, 46–53
   data protection officers, 45
   effective supervision, 48–53
   heads of department and supervisors, 40
   insurance distribution officers, 45
   legal counsel, 38–40
   management team, 37–38
   nominated officers, 45
   non-mandatory roles, 45–46
   objectives, *27–30*
   partners, 30–37
   reporting lines, 27, *27–30*
   standards, and remote working, 219–220
publicity, *104*

R v Griffiths & Pattison, 181
record maintenance, 222–223
record-keeping, 114, 118, 120
referral arrangements, 137–138
regulation, definition of, 6
regulatory compliance, 73–79, 206
   case study, 75–78
   standards, 147–152
regulatory objectives, fundamental expectations, 85–86

regulatory relationships, *104*
relationship with clients, 112
remote working, 215–217
   client identification and care
      longer-term considerations, 222–223
      short-term considerations, 221–222
   COVID-19, impact of, 217
   demonstrate response to clients' instructions, 226
   effective supervision, 225–226
   as new normal, 217–220
   and proper governance standards, 219–221
   and record maintenance, 222–223
   risk management
      dynamic response, 223
      risks, knowledge about, 223–225
resources, 235–236
retainer, 125, 127, 128–129
risk analysis documentation, 118
risk assessment, 127, 191
Risk Factors in Personal Injury Claims (warning notice), 144–145
risk management, 7, 228–229
   see also effective governance; proper governance
   considerations for, *24*
   expectations of, 17–19, 87
   remote working, 218, 223–225
Risk Outlooks, 19, *21*, 179–180
risk partners, 46
risk registry, 118
risk-based regulation, 16–19, 25, 43, 131, 148
Rosling King LLP, 36

safety messages, 66
sanctions, and money laundering, 193–194
   Emma Oettinger's insight, 194–195
self-management, 113–114
senior management, 63, 67, 169, 190–191
separate businesses, *105*
Serious Organised Crime Act 2015, 181
Solicitors Act 1974, *170*
Solicitors Disciplinary Tribunal (SDT), 41, 49, 137, 139–140, 141
   case studies, 14, 16, 20, 22–23, 75–78, 94–95, 165–166, 183–184
Solicitors Regulation Authority (SRA), 6, 9, 11–13, 153, 205
   Accounts Rules 2019, 41, 42, 120, 183, 210
   approach to compliance during COVID-19 pandemic, 218–219
   Authorisation Rules 2011, *211*
   Compensation Fund, 210
   Financial Services (Conduct of Business) Rules, 120

Index

Financial Services (Scope) Rules, 45, 120
and Legal Ombudsman, 154–155, 157–158
on money laundering, 179
new rules, *212–213*
risk determination, 18
risk management expectations, 17–19
risk priorities, 19–25, *21*, 134
  case studies, 20, 22–23
  compliance strategies, 25–27
  reporting line, 27, *27–30*
  Risk Outlooks, 19, *21*, 179–180
Risk Resource Report, 145–146
transposition of requirements, *211–212*
SRA Code of Conduct for Firms, 25, 40, 43, 48, 75, 97–98, *99–100*, 171, 172, 219, 225
  chapter 2, 25, *26–27*, 56, 148, 166, 219–220, 223
  chapter 3, 155
  chapter 4, 219, 220, 225
  contents and related managerial questions, *101–105*
SRA Code of Conduct for Solicitors, Registered European Lawyers and Registered Foreign Lawyers, 48, 97, *98–99*, 124, *132–133*, 210, 225
  chapter 7, 57, 154–155
  chapter 8, 124, 156–157, 221
SRA Handbook, 6, 23, 95, 106, 108, 135, 155–156, 209, 235
SRA Principles, 13–14, 86–87, 171, 172
  breach of, 13–14
  case studies, 14, 94–95
  changes in, 209
  practice of, 96–105
  Principle 1, *88*, *132*, 165
  Principle 2, *88*, *132*
  Principle 3, *88*, *132*, 134, 135
  Principle 4, *89*
  Principle 5, *89*, *132*, 139
  Principle 6, *90*, 143
  Principle 7, *90,* 93
SRA Standards and Regulations (STaRs), 6–7, 23, 39, 57, 74, 75, 100, 120, 172, 209
  behavioural requirements, 114
  Code of Conduct, 97
    see also **SRA Code of Conduct for Firms**; **SRA Code of Conduct for Solicitors, Registered European Lawyers and Registered Foreign Lawyers**
  definition of client, 122
  effective governance, 25
  effective supervision, 48, 52
  ethical requirements, 95, 109
  evidence in, 115
  independence principle, 136
  on integrity, 139

legal obligation, 165
Legal Ombudsman, 154
non-solicitors, 59–60
regulatory expectations in, 132–133
SRA v Malins, 140–144
Statement of Solicitor Competence, 51, 107–108, 118, 171, 172
  ethics, professionalism and judgement, 108–110
  self- and work management, 113–114
  technical legal practice, 110–112
  working with other people, 112–113
supervision, effective, 48–53, 232–233
  remote working, 225–226
  tips for, 54–56
supervision meetings
  management of, 56
  regular conduct of, 56
supervisors, role in governance structure, 40, 51–53

tax evasion offences, 182
technical legal practice, 110–112
Terrorism Act 2000, *174*, 186
third parties, *104–105*
  introductions to, *103–104*
third-party non-lawyer ownership, 136
training programmes, 117–118, 192–193
transparency, of expectations and requirements, 15
trust, 85, 86

values, 82
Vaughan, Stephen, 95, 106

Whitehouse, John, 135
  on compromise of independence, 137
  definition of independence, 135
  on independence in SRA Standards and Regulations, 136–137
  on litigation, 138
  on referral arrangements, 137–138
Wingate and Evans v SRA, 140–144
work culture, 215–216
work management, 113–114
working with other people, 112–113

Zoghbi, Valentina, 62–71

About Globe Law and Business

Globe Law and Business was established in 2005, and from the very beginning we set out to create law books which are sufficiently high level to be of real use to the experienced professional, yet still accessible and easy to navigate. Most of our authors are drawn from Magic Circle and other top commercial firms, both in the UK and internationally. Our titles are carefully produced, with the utmost attention paid to editorial, design and production processes. We hope this results in high-quality books which are easy to read, and a pleasure to own. All our new books are also available as ebooks, which are compatible with most desktop, laptop and tablet devices.

We have recently expanded our portfolio to include a new range of journals and Special Reports, available both digitally and in hard copy format, and produced to the same high standards as our books. We'd very much like to hear from you with your thoughts and ideas for improving what we offer. Please do feel free to email me at sian@globelawandbusiness.com with your views.

Sian O'Neill
Managing director
Globe Law and Business

From our Special Report series

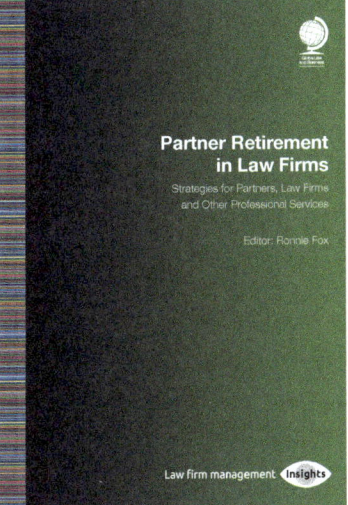

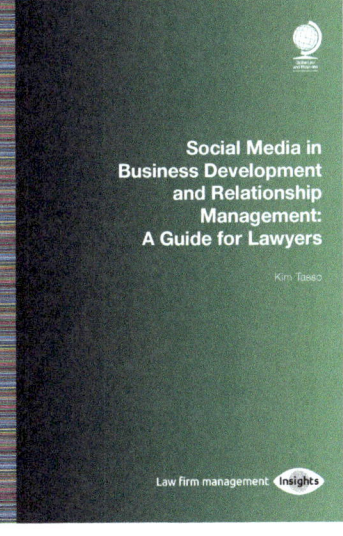

Our series of Special Reports is designed to provide you with essential information on a range of topical subjects.

Each report provides concise, accessible treatment of a key area, supported by innovative layout and design to help you absorb the information quickly and easily.

The reports are written by one or more leading authors and are underpinned by experience and research.

For full details and reviews go to **www.globelawandbusiness.com/special-reports**

Related title

Globe Law and Business

Legal Risk Management, Governance and Compliance

A Guide to Best Practice from Leading Experts
Consulting Editors **Stuart Weinstein** and **Charles Wild**

> Outside advisers, in-house counsel, or indeed auditors or managers charged in any way with implementing enlightened compliance procedures within their organisations, will welcome the practical and erudite guidance provided by this book.
>
> **Phillip Taylor MBE**
> Richmond Green Chambers

For full details and reviews go to **www.globelawandbusiness.com/LRMG**